THE VICTORIOUS LIFE
OF *Faith*

DR. RICHARD B. PEOPLES, SR.

Order this book online at www.trafford.com
or email orders@trafford.com

Most Trafford titles are also available at major online book retailers.

Print information available on the last page.

ISBN: 978-1-4907-7722-1 (sc)
ISBN: 978-1-4907-7724-5 (hc)
ISBN: 978-1-4907-7723-8 (e)

Library of Congress Control Number: 2016917304

MSG
Scripture quotations marked MSG are taken from The Message. © 1993,
1994, 1995, 1996, 2000, 2001, 2002, 2003 by Eugene H. Peterson.
Used by permission of NavPress Publishing Group. Website.

NCV
Scripture quotations marked NCV are taken from the New Century
Version, © 1987, 1988, 1991 by Word Publishing, a division of Thomas
Nelson, Inc. Used by permission. All rights reserved.

AMP
Scripture quotations marked AMP are from The Amplified Bible, Old Testament. ©
1965, 1987 by the Zondervan Corporation. The Amplified Bible, New Testament © 1954,
1958, 1987 by the Lockman Foundation. Used by permission. All rights reserved.

TLB
Scripture quotations marked TLB are taken from The Living Bible. © 1971. Used by
permission of Tyndale House Publishers, Inc., Carol Stream, Illinois 60188. All rights reserved.

Trafford rev.   10/17/2016

 www.trafford.com

North America & international
toll-free: 1 888 232 4444 (USA & Canada)
fax: 812 355 4082

CONTENTS

FOREWORD

I am honored that Pastor Richard Peoples, Sr. would ask me to write the foreword for his book, *The Victorious Life of Faith*. I have known this man for many years, and he is a precious brother in the faith. Through the years, I have watched Pastor Peoples faithfully carry out the vision God gave him for the city of Augusta. A respected leader in our city, he demonstrates the goodness and faithfulness of God as he lives a life full of faith and victory: he walks the walk and talks the talk.

Throughout his book, Pastor Peoples presents a foundational principle of Christianity: faith. The Scriptures teach us that the Lord has supernaturally empowered us to go further in our walk of faith. Pastor Peoples goes beyond presenting just another teaching on faith. His message is clear and profound: the victorious life is one soundly rooted and grounded in a trust in God. It is having an unshakable confidence that says, "Regardless of the situation or circumstance, God will not only bring us through, but we will rise as victors and champions!" This book can help transform your life and bring you to a deeper and more profound understanding of faith in Him. You will be inspired, blessed, and enriched as you read this wonderful book.

Dr. Sandra G. Kennedy
Founder and Senior Pastor
Whole Life Ministries, Inc., Augusta, Georgia

Bishop Richard B. Peoples, Sr., who is and has been my spiritual father for over twenty years, has taught me and demonstrated to countless believers in the body of Christ that we are people of faith. We are saved by faith, we walk by faith, we live by faith, we pray with faith, we believe God by faith, and we read the scriptures to obtain faith. The carnal mind seeks to lean us towards living in the natural realm only, but as believers there is also a spiritual realm, and Bishop Peoples teaches, through this book, that faith sees beyond the natural realm into the spiritual realm, and it rises to every challenge and overcomes every obstacle. Everything in the Christian walk comes by faith and, as we feed on the word of God, which builds our faith, we begin to develop greater faith. This is a must-read book for all believers within the Body of Christ.

Jonathan D. Bryant Sr.
Pastor, Resurrection Christian Life Center Middleburg, Florida

I think one of the most important things that the church can talk about today is in the area of faith. We've tried all kinds of things in the church to help believers grow in the area of their faith with very little success. I believe it is because we have made something that should be simple unnecessarily difficult to understand and comprehend. Thus many people are literally cut off from their faith, and they are unable to realize their spirit is calling out for more.

Dr. Richard Peoples is a masterful teacher and literary artist. Aside from leading two ministry campuses and overseeing several churches, Dr. Peoples understands faith and how to transform words of faith into tangible manifestations of God. In *The Victorious Life of Faith*, Dr. Peoples makes a call for people to challenge themselves by embracing the various dynamics of faith rather than shrinking back in fear and disbelief. In addition, he reveals everything from the elementary principle of "What Is Faith" to the life-changing dynamics of "Faith for Life."

This book will empower the believer to discover a greater level of confidence in their ability to apply the principles and practices of faith. When this happens, many people will begin to spiritually train like a boxer to achieve the "The Unbeatable Spirit of Faith." This is "More Precious than Gold," as they begin to stretch out in their faith.

If the reader applies this capsulated miracle of faith so illustriously illustrated with simplicity, accuracy, and enlightened understanding, their lives will never be the same.

Rosetta Parker-Austin, MEd, LPC
Author, From the Eyes of a Seer, and A2S 2016

I have enjoyed an amazing journey walking with Christ for over two decades. It has been a journey defined by God's grace and my faith. Grasping the enormity of God's tireless dedication to me and the plans He made for me before the world began is refreshingly liberating. I have a God who loves me unconditionally and who chooses to use me by His unearned and amazing grace. If grace is one side of coin of my life's journey, the other side is faith. What God does for, in, with, and through me, He unquestionably does by grace. But my response to His grace is not grace but rather faith. God does what He does by grace, and He requires me to do what I do by faith. The Bible does not call or command us to live by grace. The Bible is clear, in both call and commandment, that we are to live by faith.

Much of what I know about faith I learned from Pastor Richard Peoples. He taught me by both precept and example. In this book, you will read many of the lessons He has taught me in person. You will read the words. I have had the blessed privilege of reading the person. My prayer for you is that the lessons of faith outlined in this book have the same impact on you as they have had on me. I am who I am by God's grace. I have enjoyed an amazing life in Christ living by faith.

Read the lessons. Open your heart to hear the voice behind the voice and the Word behind the words, and use your faith to access God's grace. Living this way, you will become the man or woman God called you to be, and you will leave a mark in this world that will not be easily erased.

Rick Piña
President and Founder
Rick & Isabella Piña Ministries

It is always a great honor to read books that have been tried and proven by the writer. Bishop Richard Peoples is one of those leaders of the Gospel of a rare breed who writes from the experience of life. He has proven these principles in his own life and ministry and seen through his faith and patience the manifestations of God's power. *The Victorious Life of Faith* can also change your life if you put the principles in this book into practice. The information provided in this book is a great resource for the person seeking victory over the challenges of life or the pastor who has vision but not enough faith and can't see that his/her victory is just on the horizon.

The importance of a book like this cannot be overstated. The information contained in these pages have the power to give you access to the power of FAITH. It is the master key to unlock the doors of opportunity when you operate by the God kind of faith. I will advise every person that reads this book to absorb not only the content in this book, but the spirit of its author and to enter into a life of victorious faith.

Whether you are going through a hard time and need faith to overcome, or if you just want to know how to take your faith to a level of guaranteed victory – no matter what, this book is for you.

Prepare yourself for a total life changing makeover.

Wanta Ezell
Co-Pastor, World Covenant Christian Center, Conyers, Georgia

ACKNOWLEDGEMENTS

As I consider everyone who has invested into my life, which was the training ground for this work, I realize there are far too many to thank individually. However, I would be amiss if I did not express my earnest and sincere appreciation to my wife, Janice Peoples. We have walked this walk since 1977 and so often it has been your encouragement and support that has given me the desire to keep moving forward. To my children, Janeice, Richard Jr., Altomesha, and Anthony, it has been my joy to see you enter into *The Victorious Life of Faith*. It is through you that I have come to understand the heart of the Father.

To the administrative staff of Faith Outreach Church, Marcelino Sanchez, Jr., Kerstin Edwards, Larry Jackson, and Whitney Jones, your professionalism, cover and support speaks volumes of your heart for God. I am humbled by your loyalty. A special note of gratitude to Sabrina Sanchez; daughter you grabbed the heart of this work and I am grateful. To every leader, member, past and present and every teacher and mentor, thank you. The crossing of our lives has caused me to embrace and radically pursue *The Victorious Life of Faith*.

Finally and most importantly, Father in the name of Jesus, thank You for choosing and trusting me to be Your voice in all the earth. I am forever captured by your love and your will.

INTRODUCTION

What you have in your hand has the potential to change your entire life! I believe that with all of my heart. I do not say that to be arrogant or puffed up in myself, quite the contrary. I boldly make that statement because of my absolute confidence in God, the finished work of Jesus Christ on Calvary, and the ever present Holy Spirit. They give me the confidence; it is upon Them I squarely place my faith—and faith is what this work is all about.

The next one hundred–plus pages are filled with what I consider to be some key foundational and life applicable truths that I have received from God in the past twenty-five years. These are not vague concepts and ideas that I heard about at a conference. I am sharing with you the heart of what God has shared with me. Not only did He share these truths and vital life points, I have continually used them in my life, marriage, family, and ministry. After all, when God gives you instructions in success, it would be foolish to not employ them.

I have discovered absolutely nothing in the Kingdom of God operates successfully apart from faith. I truly believe that faith is the deciding factor in a believer's life that determines if they live a victorious life. Sometimes we get so caught up on the need for "perfection" or the exact order of the "steps to success." God's Word is not difficult, and perfection is not a requirement. The more I study the Word of God the clearer it becomes to me; faith in God is paramount to success.

Now, I am not talking about the "name it and claim it" type of faith. We will discuss that later in one of the chapters. I am talking about faith that is mature enough to go take possession of what the grace of God has made available. I am talking about faith that is a way of life, everyday life.

I have purposefully made this easy to read, intertwining my own experiences to help encourage and stimulate the growth of faith in your life. It is my prayer that each one of you reading *The Victorious Life of Faith* will get a clearer understanding of the "God kind of faith" and then you will begin to apply that understanding to your life. Let me tell you something right here, God loves you, and He wants you to live in victory! Would He send His Son to die so you could live in defeat? You were already living there! God wants you to be victorious; He wants you to walk boldly into the future He has predestined for you! God wants you to be free of sickness, free of debt, free of lack . . . He wants you to be free indeed! Your faith is the key vehicle that will get you to that place; faith in God.

Get your pencil, a good study Bible, and find yourself a quiet spot; God is about to transform your life as your faith explodes! Enjoy the fireworks.

CHAPTER 1

Experiencing the Victorious Life of Faith

*"The thief comes only in order to steal and kill and destroy.
I came that they may have and enjoy life, and have it in
abundance (to the full, till it overflows)." John 10:10 (AMP)*

I am convinced that as Christians, we are supposed to have life, not just merely exist, and we are to enjoy that life, taking delight and pleasure in it. It is not meant for us to walk around or live life sad, mad, depressed, discouraged, miserable, hurt, and upset all the time; there is no victory in that kind of living. That is not the life that Jesus said He came to give to us. When we chose or made Jesus the Lord of our lives, we chose life in the absolute sense.

I grew up in an era when people believed enduring more pain and having more problems were signs of being more spiritual. Now that I am more mature in Christ, I know that is not true. In fact, the truth of the matter is your relationship with God should cause your life to be more enjoyable and more victorious. Not to say that the life of a Christian will be pain and problem free, but in the midst of challenges, it is your relationship with God that should cause you to continue enjoying your life in Christ. Surrendering to God brings victory and opens an enjoyable life before you! You know joy is supposed to be a mark of Christianity because it is a manifestation of the Fruit of the Spirit. If God is working in your life, you ought to be a joyful person—someone who faces the worst day and still has joy.

As you are enjoying your life, the greatest joy should come from your relationship with Jesus. Of course, to enjoy a relationship you have to spend time together. As you spend time with God and you begin to really enjoy your relationship with Him, you will begin to experience greater joy and victories in your marriage, with your children, in your church family, on your jobs, and every other area of your life. Simply stated, you will begin to experience victorious living! You cannot spend time with Jesus and your life not be changed. Acts 4:13 makes that clear: *"The leaders saw that Peter and John were not afraid to speak, and they understood that these men had no special training or education. So they were amazed. Then they realized that Peter and John had been with Jesus"* (NCV).

As you begin to live a victorious life, do you know what will happen? First of all, others will see it. You have seen them, those people who, no matter what, live in victory, walking in faith, enjoying the journey. Just as you see it on others—people can see it on you! Once others see you living that victorious life, do you know what happens next? People will be drawn to you. Well actually they will not be drawn to you; they will be drawn to the confident, faith-filled life of victory you are living! When I was a little boy back in Slocomb, Alabama, we loved to find those old televisions thrown out. We would get into the back of the box and pull out the magnet; then we would walk around using that magnet to pick up nails and other metal objects. Those old magnets were great attractors. God wants your life to be a great attractor, drawing others into the kingdom of God. It is not easy to tell people how great and loving your God is if you are never enjoying life. You should be embracing the life of God by enjoying day to day living.

Notice what Jesus said in John 10:10 (MSG): *"A thief is only there to steal and kill and destroy. I came so they can have real and eternal life, more and better life than they ever dreamed of."* Jesus said that He came so we can have "life." The word "life" used here is the Greek word "zoe", which means "life in the absolute sense, life as God has it."[1] That is real and genuine life! Not life based on what you have, what is given, or what circumstances and situations you are facing, but life based on Christ's finished work on Calvary, life based on God's goodness and His riches! Now that is good news, not just for you but for others as well.

Individually and collectively, as a church we ought to reflect a culture that is living and experiencing the victorious life of faith! Our churches should foster an environment that is fun and inviting; a place where people are growing spiritually. The Church should be a reflection of Christ. The Church should be a place where people can come and experience the life and love of God through us. If we are really experiencing life in all of its fullness, it is going to show up on us in an enjoyable way, and it is going to draw others.

There are three principal ways of really experiencing the victorious life of faith that I want to share with you.

FIRST

LOVE LIFE. You should live life loving and enjoying the life that we have. You should not allow people or circumstances to hinder us from loving life! You have to get to a place that you do not allow what we face externally to affect and infect us internally. John 15:11 says, *"I have told you this so that my joy may be in you and that your joy may be complete."* God wants His joy in you! Jesus enjoyed life, and as His disciples, you should be embracing the personality and example of Jesus and learning to love life.

Have you ever been around or maybe you have been a person who is always complaining and never enjoying life? Some people let a bad encounter in life keep them from forgiving, loving, and enjoying life. That type of thinking does not make any more sense than allowing one bad encounter at Wal-Mart keep you from going back to the store. Most of us would get over that negative incident and return to the store the next day. You must learn to do the same in life, not allowing the negative to build up, causing you to become haters of life instead of lovers of life. Let me explain it this way, whatever you magnify will become larger and the decision is always yours—magnify the Lord or magnify the negative. Personally, not only do I refuse to magnify the negative, I just cannot sit still around people who want to sit and dig a hole complaining about what they are going through. I just have to help them to talk about the goodness of God to help them to choose to use their words for life not death.

In 2 Corinthians 6, Paul told the church of Corinth in every way, in every manner he lives his life in such a way that others see that he is a servant of God. He then went on to share highs and lows of living but ended in verse 10 saying, *"...sorrowful, yet always rejoicing; poor, yet making many rich; having nothing, and yet possessing everything."* The Apostle Paul discovered the joy of loving life. His faith and confidence was placed squarely on God not on himself and not on his circumstances. Church, I want that. You have to embrace the personality of Jesus and really love life to experience the victorious life of faith.

SECOND

To really experience the victorious life of faith, you are going to have to **LOVE PEOPLE.** As Christians, we are to be known for loving people. What did Jesus say in John 13:35? *"Your strong love for each other will prove to the world that you are my disciples"* (TLB). You cannot enjoy life if you despise people, and you cannot pretend to love people. 1 John 3:18 (TLB) takes away our "pretend rights," *"Little children, let us stop just saying we love people; let us really love them, and show it by our actions."*

The problem is a lot of you have let people get up under your skin, irritating you. People who are hurt tend to hurt others, and many of you had been on the receiving end of that pain. The truth is you are not enjoying your life right now because you do not like people. Hurt at the hands of others happens to everyone. Pain and hurt are legitimate emotions caused by disappointment or offense.

Now, you may not be able to control when pain and hurt come, but you can control your response to the hurt; it is within your power to choose how you respond. It is your choice. The choice is to hold the offender captive or to let them go. 1 Peter 3:10 (AMP) reminds you of the position God commands believers to take: *"For let him who wants to enjoy life and see good days [good—whether apparent or not] keep his tongue free from evil and his lips from guile (treachery, deceit)."*

If you want to experience the victorious life of faith, you must stop letting your heart become polluted by people—instead love them. When you choose to withhold unconditional love and forgiveness, you are jeopardizing your ability to enjoy life. You must love people, believe in them, and accept them. Do not worry about keeping score. Free yourself from the heavy weight of carrying around what others have done to you. Give yourself permission to enjoy life by loving people.

THIRD

Finally, to truly experience the victorious life of faith that Jesus secured you must **LOVE GOD.** You cannot do this "Christian thing" without a deep love for God, it just will not work. Oh, it will work for a little while, but the real acid test will show you up. When God tells you to love people who have hurt you—you will not be able to obey if you do not love Him. When life is not lovable because trouble is breaking out on every side you will not be able to obey Him if you do not love Him. Do you recall what Jesus said in John 14:15? He said, *"If you [really] love Me, you will keep and obey My commandments"* (AMP). That is pretty plain: "if you **really** love Me . . ." Loving God is vital to living victoriously. The second part of that Scripture reveals the level of love you have for Him will be reflected in your obedience!

To some people, that might seem like a hard thing to do, but when you truly encounter and begin to live for your awesome God, loving and obeying Him will become automatic, like breathing.

With everything in me, I love the Lord, and I know the fact that I enjoy life so much is directly connected to the love I have for Him and most importantly the love He has for me!

Everything you do in ministry should be done out of your love for God, not performing as a duty or show. I challenge you to change the way you look at your responsibilities and obligations within ministry from "I <u>have</u> to do" to "I <u>get</u> to do". What an honor, I get to spend time with God, reading His Word and praying! I get to serve others and lead them to the source of joy I have found in Christ Jesus! What an honor; I do not "have to" I "get to" do these things—I am privileged to do all He has called me to do and become all He has destined me to become!

God desires that you have life in the absolute sense, enjoying it to the fullest. People often do not enjoy life because they pull against God and His plans. To me that is just as smart as pulling against a self-propelled lawn mower; the lawn mower pulling one way and you pulling the other. I have found that cooperating with God always brings the greatest results. Ecclesiastes 2:24–25 (NCV) explains it best: *"The best that people can do is eat, drink, and enjoy their work. I saw that even this comes from God, because no one can eat or enjoy life without him."* No one can really enjoy life without God.

When Janice and I got married, I was a young soldier in the Army with pockets so empty I had to borrow money from Trans American Loan Company to get married. However, I told her one day I would take her to Jamaica and the Bahamas. I wanted to bless my bride, and there is nothing wrong with that. Twenty years later, God revealed His plan to bless us both and our trip together was greater than anything I could have planned or paid for on my own! He continually shows Janice and I over and over again that He wants us to enjoy life to the fullest!

I love life. I love people. I love God. I love living in victory. I love living this victorious life of faith!

Think About It

1. The results of your life, your relationship with Christ should be an inviting welcome to others.

2. To experience the victorious life of faith, you must love life, people, and God.

3. Everything you do in ministry should be done out of your love for God.

4. God wants you to enjoy life!

Personal Notes

CHAPTER 2

What Is Faith?

"Now faith is the assurance (title deed, confirmation) of things hoped for (divinely guaranteed), and the evidence of things not seen [the conviction of their reality—faith comprehends as fact what cannot be experienced by the physical senses]." Hebrews 11:1 (AMP)

"What is Faith?" That is an explosive question with so many possible responses. I get excited just thinking about answers to that question! Let me give you a natural explanation of faith. When I was a little boy growing up in Slocomb, Alabama, in the early 1960s, no matter what I saw or heard, I just knew my Daddy and Mama would always take care of us; and in the mind of that little boy, there was no limit to what they could and would do. I was confident in that fact. They loved their children and everyone knew that truth. However, as I grew older, I began to understand their care and protection <u>was</u> limited, no matter how much they loved; their desire to care and protect was bordered and boxed in by their ability. Now, when I accepted Christ as my Savior and began to learn about His limitless abilities; when I learned nothing is impossible for God and that He is omnipresent, omnipotent, omniscient; when I learned that God loves me with an everlasting love, He always has and always will love me, something began to stir within me. As I continued to study the Bible, putting into action what I was learning, I began to connect that new information to what I had learned from my parents, and something greater began to stir within me! I discovered the great awakening within was faith! Faith exploded within, quickening me, and affecting every aspect of my life. I began to trust in the one true God, the One who is not limited by anything! If I could find it in the Bible, I knew I could trust it to be true—through confidently trusting my parents, I was prepared to learn to trust my God!

NO FAITH ~ NO VICTORY

I learned nothing works in the Kingdom of God without faith; it is the currency of the Kingdom of God. It is a principal element needed if you are to live victoriously and do great exploits. **Salvation** is not possible without it. **Healing** and **victory** are impossible without it. **Prosperity** cannot be obtained without it. **Success** in any area is only possible when you are living or operating in faith. Faith is so powerful and crucial in the life of believers that Scripture says God cannot be pleased without it. Hebrews 11:6 (KJV) says, *"But without faith it is impossible to please him: for he that cometh to God must believe that he is, and that he is a rewarder of them that diligently seek him."* I learned no faith, no victory, and I learned that lesson very quickly! You see victory is important to me.

FAITH IS . . .

So let's look at a few basic "what is faith" answers. **Faith is . . .**

- **A practical expression of your confidence in God and His Word.** Faith believes that God IS and not that He WAS. It believes that He is able AND willing to do. Faith is believing what God says about your circumstances in life rather than accepting as fact what you see, feel, and hear. You know satan's whole objective in life is to attack your confidence in God's Word; trying to make you believe God is not going to do what He promised. Your faith and confidence in God and His Word will raise you above the enemy's attacks. In other words, your life and your actions will reflect or express, in practical ways, your confidence in God and His Word.

- **Faith is the producer of good reports.** When you operate in faith, it brings God on the scene, freeing Him to move on your behalf. It is your access to the power of God connecting you to your God-given ability to get results. Faith commands blessings. When God is involved in anything, you know the end result will be victory, and that is the making of good reports.

- **Your means of pleasing God.** Your perusing faith in Jesus is what pleases God. This is not natural human faith; it is supernatural. This type of faith grasps the "impossibilities" of hope and brings them into reality. Looking at Hebrews 11:1, you can see that hope is the blueprint for what you believe, but faith "fills" hope with substance, and that is pleasing to God. Later, in the same chapter, God clearly declares without faith He is not pleased.[2]

- **A way of life.** Faith is not something you try out to see if it works for you like a new business venture. Faith is a way of life that is lived; when it is easy as well as when it is difficult. For every believer who is determined to live a victorious life, faith must be the foundation of your living. Four times in the Bible God declares, *"The just shall live by faith."*[3] Faith is not a movement or a denomination, faith is the way believers are commanded to live.

- **Now, substance and evidence.** Let's look at Hebrews 11:1 (KJV): *"Now faith is the substance of things hoped for, the evidence of things not seen."* Notice, first of all that faith is always **now** or in the present tense, not tomorrow or yesterday, it is now. Second, faith is the **substance**. It is the ground or foundation (confident, assurance, certainty, or confirmation) of things you hope for or are expecting. Hope is what you are looking for in the future. It is a goal setter, but your faith goes and gets it. Think about the times you hoped and prayed for something to happen, but you never attached your active faith to your hope. Did you ever accomplish what you were hoping for? Probably not until you attached your active faith. Your faith, working for you, went out and acquired what your hope alone could not obtain. <u>Third</u>, faith is the **evidence** (proof) of things not seen. Think about it, faith is now, and if you have it now, you have the evidence of its existence. You do not have to wait for a physical manifestation of what your faith has already confirmed and verified. Faith is now, faith is substance, and faith is evidence.

- **A barrier breaker.** So many are living life within limits that God did not set. Living a life of faith will break and destroy all barriers set by the enemy, others, and even those set by you. Faith in God and His Word will cause you to believe so much more than your natural senses can comprehend. Natural logic may say go north, but when you are living by faith and receive a word from God that says go south, nothing will deter you; your focus will be set south to victory! Barriers erected by others will be destroyed as the truth of God's Word is received and believed. You see you might have been told your whole life you are a mistake and worthless, but sir, ma'am, when you begin to have greater faith in what God says about you, the barriers will be destroyed!

- **An invisible force that comes out of our human spirit that can literally move mountains.** Remember in Matthew 17 when the disciples asked Jesus why they were limited in their ability? Jesus replied, *"Because you have so little faith. Truly I tell you, if you have faith as small as a mustard seed, you can say to this mountain, 'Move from here to there,' and it will move. Nothing will be impossible for you."*[4] They lacked faith— faith that produces power and anointing. Faith that enables you to do what you otherwise could never accomplish. While people will never see your faith, they will see the works of your faith moving mountains!

FAITH IS NOT . . .

While I do not want to invest a lot of time in this area, I sense a need to briefly share a few faith misconceptions. **Faith is not** . . .

- **Mental assent.** You can mentally agree with the Word of God, but until you believe it with your heart, having an inner image of the Word coming to pass in your life, your faith is not in operation. Until your belief moves you to action beyond thinking, your faith is not in operation. You can quote Scripture all day long, but if you do not believe what you are saying, you are not operating in faith. Mental assent is not faith.

- **Perceived with your five physical senses.** In Romans 4:17, God declares that He calls into existence things that are not seen. Your natural senses cannot comprehend your faith. When a believer's body is racked with pain, and they declare healing the mind will be confused and will fight against the spirit. Faith is often contrary to the natural, but faith is the victory! Waiting to see it is not faith, Thomas (John 20:24–29).

- **Name it and claim it.** You know the "name it and claim it" movement did more to devalue the concept of faith than many realize. It took a vital foundational part of God's plan for His children and reduced it to laying hands on objects and declaring ownership. At its core, it was an attempt to make a mockery of God's plan, but God will never be mocked. His children, as they sought a greater understanding of His Word, soon understood the difference. You cannot use your "faith" to get what God never intended you to possess. Manipulation is not faith.

- **The answer to defeat.** As God's child, you are not the defeated one trying to get victory by your faith. You are a victorious over comer through your faith. You already have the victory! The victorious life of faith is secured—it is yours!

GOD'S PLAN

I believe learning, understanding, embracing, and living a life of faith is the greatest plank in the foundation of every believer. The presence or absence of faith will determine victory or defeat. To live by faith is God's desire for you because His plan is that we live in victory.

Let's go forward to learn more about God's plan for you to live a victorious life of faith.

Think About It

1. Nothing in the Kingdom of God operates apart from faith.

2. Where your faith is lacking so your victories will lack as well.

3. You cannot please God without faith.

4. Living by faith will move you into action. No Action – No Faith.

Personal Notes

CHAPTER 3

Confidence—The Missing Ingredient

"For the LORD shall be thy confidence, and shall keep thy foot from being taken." Proverbs 3:26 (KJV)

My sister-in-law, Jackie, makes the best pound cake I have ever tasted. I am not just saying that because she is my sister-in-law. Anyone who has ever tasted her cake will tell you the same thing. While she will not share her recipe, I know she has one, and she is adamant that every ingredient is vital. She will not attempt to bake it without all of the ingredients on her secret list. She has learned, to create that mouth-watering circle of goodness, to obtain great success, she must include all of the ingredients.

The same concept is true in your life as you endeavor to live the victorious life of faith that Jesus has already secured for us. Many Christians are failing and frustrated in their attempts to live in victory, and that was never God's intent. Often, the missing ingredient in the life of these frustrated believers is confidence.

Confidence is a major key element or ingredient in your faith walk. When you are speaking and confessing the Scriptures, you must be sure that you believe what you are saying; that is confidence. Confidence is "the belief that one can rely on someone or something; a firm trust."[5] True and unshakable confidence in God and His Word is being fully persuaded, no matter what the circumstances look like. Amid every situation, confidence declares the outcome will be what God spoke at the beginning.

CONFIDENCE = BOLDNESS

When the Bible uses the word **confidence** it means "assurance" or complete and total "persuasion". It also closely parallels the meaning of "trust". When you trust something or someone, you have confidence in it. Another term directly identified with confidence is "boldness". In fact, boldness can often be used interchangeably with confidence.

Proverbs 3:26 (KJV) says, *"The Lord shall be thy confidence, and shall keep thy foot from being taken."* God Himself is to be your confidence and your assurance. You can always count on God to do exactly what He says. Just knowing that God has your back, and that He is going to keep you as you step out in faith, should increase your confidence and give you great boldness!

Confidence is the quality that will lead you to stand up under and endure adversity. It causes you to undertake a difficult task with diligence. Take a look at 1 Samuel 17. The Word of God says when King Saul and his warriors heard Goliath taunting them *"Saul and all the Israelites were dismayed and terrified"* (v.11); they lacked confidence. You will never take a firm stand for anything without confidence. For forty days, this "Philistine champion" bullied the army of Israel; he actually had them running.

Then one day, David, the shepherd boy, was sent to take food to his brothers on the front lines. When David saw what was going on, he took action. He understood his covenant with God, and he knew that Goliath was not under the same covenant. David's history with God strengthened his boldness. He proclaimed God had delivered him from the claws of the lion and the bear, and that victorious history gave David the assurance that God would give him victory over this enemy. As the shepherd boy approached the giant on the battlefield, Goliath, dressed in his battle armor, mocked and cursed David and his God. I love David's bold response, a response that came from his absolute confidence in God. *"David said to the Philistine, 'You come against me with sword and spear and javelin, but*

I come against you in the name of the Lord Almighty, the God of the armies of Israel, whom you have defied. This day the Lord will deliver you into my hands, and I'll strike you down and cut off your head. This very day I will give the carcasses of the Philistine army to the birds and the wild animals, and the whole world will know that there is a God in Israel. All those gathered here will know that it is not by sword or spear that the Lord saves; for the battle is the Lord's, and he will give all of you into our hands" (1 Samuel 17:45–47).

Do you know what happened next? Exactly what David said! *"As the Philistine moved closer to attack him, David ran quickly toward the battle line to meet him. Reaching into his bag and taking out a stone, he slung it and struck the Philistine on the forehead. The stone sank into his forehead, and he fell face-down on the ground. So David triumphed over the Philistine with a sling and a stone; without a sword in his hand he struck down the Philistine and killed him. David ran and stood over him. He took hold of the Philistine's sword and drew it from the sheath. After he killed him, he cut off his head with the sword"* (1 Samuel 17:48–51). David was totally persuaded! He possessed complete confidence and trust in God!

THE VALUE OF CONFIDENCE

Let me share something with you, when you no longer have confidence in the Word of God, you stop the manifestation you desire from it. Keep in mind confidence is developed over a period of time. Many times, when trouble comes your way, it is satan's attack on your confidence. Satan attacks your confidence because he does not want you to believe that the Word of God works. He wants to fill you with doubt and uncertainty.

You have to take heed to what the writer of Hebrews said in Hebrews 10:35 (AMP) *"Do not, therefore, fling away your [fearless] confidence, for it has a glorious and great reward."* In other words, do not dismiss, dump, or discard your confidence—do not throw it away. Now thinking and acting in line with that, scripture will oppose the way the "flesh" thinks and will often be contrary to what your eyes see, but your confidence must be solid in what God says. Do not let what is before you that is contrary to what God declares shake your confidence and rattle your faith.

Like the Apostle Paul, I want to challenge believers to have confidence in God. In Philippians 1:6 (MSG), he said, "*There has never been the slightest doubt in my mind that the God who started this great work in you would keep at it and bring it to a flourishing finish on the very day Christ Jesus appears.*" God is faithful! You just have to settle that within yourself. Numbers 23:19 (AMPC) reveals "*God is not a man, that He should tell or act a lie, neither the son of man, that He should feel repentance or compunction [for what He has promised]. Has He said and shall He not do it? Or has He spoken and shall He not make it good?*" God is faithful to His Word. His earnest desire is that you experience the full manifestation of every promise in His Word. The more you believe, the more you trust God and the more your confidence will grow.

THE LOOK OF CONFIDENCE

May I show you what confidence looks like? "*Though the fig tree does not bud and there are no grapes on the vines, though the olive crop fails and the fields produce no food, though there are no sheep in the pen and no cattle in the stalls, yet I will rejoice in the LORD, I will be joyful in God my Savior*" (Habakkuk 3:17–18). That is what confidence and trust looks like. Habakkuk says even if my crops fail, livestock is destroyed, and nothing is going right, there is still one response . . . "*yet will I rejoice in the Lord, I will be joyful in God my Savior.*" How could he be so optimistic in the face of incredible adversity? You have to read verse 19 to understand: "*The Sovereign Lord is my strength; he makes my feet like the feet of a deer, he enables me to tread on the heights.*" He was confident that the Lord is sovereign, He is Lord, and He will cause certain and complete victory!

WIN OR QUIT

Remember, it is not over until you either win or quit. Like Habakkuk, you have to make sure your confidence is not dependent on your surroundings and circumstances but on the Lord! You must have faith in God; your faith in Him is a practical expression of the confidence you have in Him. It is just this simple . . .

Great Faith = Great Confidence
Little Faith = Little Confidence

HOLD ON

Once you have developed confidence in a promise of God, the next thing you must do is to hold on to that promise. Hebrews 3:14 says, *"For we are made partakers of Christ, if we hold the beginning of our confidence steadfast unto the end"* (KJV). If you want to receive the promises of God in your life, you must hold tightly to your confidence until the end. When is the end you ask? When you have the manifestation of the promise in which you have placed your confidence—that is the end. Do not faint, do not quit, and do not give up your confidence.

"Well, Pastor Peoples, what do I do when I get tired, when I get weary?" Brothers and sisters, I am here to tell you we all get tired, and we all get weary. It is in those times I have found that as I draw near to Him, trusting in His goodness, His faithfulness, and His Word, that He strengthens and renews me and my faith. The Holy Spirit reminds me of the victories God has led me through. He helps me look past the situation before me to see the matchless wonder of who God is, and my confidence is revitalized!

Your faith needs your confidence, and you need your faith to live this victorious life!

Think About It

1. No matter what challenges you face, when your confidence is squarely and completely on God, you will not be shaken.

2. Without confidence in God, you will waver, become terrified and ultimately be defeated by the adversity that SEEMS invincible.

3. When you become weary, draw near to God. He is there to be the source of your strength.

4. Without regard to what is before you, have confidence in Who is behind you—hold on to the promises of God.

Personal Notes

CHAPTER 4

Faith Is the Victory

"For everyone born of God is victorious and overcomes the world; and this is the victory that has conquered and overcome the world—our [continuing, persistent] faith [in Jesus the Son of God]." 1 John 5:4 (AMP)

Now that you understand the connection between your confidence and your faith, I want to make a life changing declaration—**Faith is the Believer's Victory**! Look at 1 John 5:4–5 in the Message Bible: *"Every God-begotten person conquers the world's ways. The conquering power that brings the world to its knees is our faith. The person who wins out over the world's ways is simply the one who believes Jesus is the Son of God."* Do you see that? You have access to the conquering power that will bring the world (this system) to its knees! Sickness, lack, brokenness, low self-esteem—all of it to its knees! When you put your confidence in the Word, faith becomes your victory. Can it be that easy? Yes ma'am, yes sir, it is that easy. Your faith in God will always lead you down the path of victory. Let's look at 2 Corinthians 2:14 for Bible proof to that truth: *"But thanks be to God, who always leads us in triumph in Christ, and through us spreads and makes evident everywhere the sweet fragrance of the knowledge of Him"* (AMP). He always leads us to victory; unfortunately, we do not always follow His lead. However, I believe God is changing that right now, and you are becoming a better follower, in the name of Jesus!

Let's examine 1 John 5:4–5 from the King James Version: *"For whatsoever is born of God overcometh the world: and this is the victory that overcometh the world, even our faith. Who is he that overcometh the world, but he that believeth that Jesus is the Son of God?"* Notice it says "this is <u>THE</u> victory" it does not say this is <u>A</u> victory. Faith is the victory that overcomes the world—social struggles, poverty, failing marriages, problems with your children—there is no limit to the power of your faith! When anything seems to be subduing, overcoming, and bringing you under its control, that is an indication that you have not built up your faith in that area of your life because where faith is present, it subdues everything contrary to God's Word.

ALREADY VICTORIOUS

May I tell you something? As a believer you are not fighting the good fight of faith to obtain victory; you are fighting from the position of already having victory! I am not trying to obtain my victory, in fact, the real truth is the enemy is trying to obtain my victory; he wants to steal it from me or better yet deceive me into giving it up! However, I found out once I fixed my focus on faith in God and His Word, there is absolutely nothing the enemy can do except wear himself out trying to rob what Jesus already secured for me— *VICTORY!*

Four times in the Bible, God declares "the just shall live by faith."[6] No matter what is going on around you, as a Disciple of Christ, faith is the substance that should be coming out of you. When you are living by faith, fixed faith, even when difficulty shows up, the response will be raising your sights above the situation and refocusing on God. When circumstances surface beyond control that is when what you really believe will surface as well. The depth of your faith in God's character and promises will become evident, as well as your doubts and uncertainties. To abide in God's will and live in victory will require a steady, trust-filled focus on Him in the challenging moments as well as in the moments of celebration.

While God does not bring calamity on you, He will use those times as opportunities to help you grow and deepen your faith, as well as the faith of others. Look at the transitioning life of Joseph throughout Genesis. Loved by his father, hated by his brothers, Joseph dreamed dreams given to him by God. His brothers sold him into slavery. However, amid the treachery and bondage, he refused to become bitter; he continued to trust God and continued to keep his faith focused on God. The entire time, even when falsely accused and imprisoned, Joseph kept his focus centered on the Lord who caused him to flourish against all odds; Joseph recognized and acknowledged God's constant presence. As a result of his steadfast confidence in God, he earned promotions and ultimately was the tool God used to rescue his family. It was Joseph's faith that obtained the victory for him, God's people, and God Himself!

YOUR FAITH STRENGTHENS OTHERS

Your life of faith will not only bring victory for you, but for others as they witness the testimony of how good God is in your life. As you speak in faith concerning a situation that seems hopeless others are listening; some in disbelief, some in "want to believe" and some in faith. When your faith brings about the victory, and you give all glory and honor to God, all three groups of listeners are affected as they see your faith, placed squarely on God, in action. Now, of course, you must believe what you say when you say it; that is opposite of the "Thomas faith," who had to see it to believe.[7] In Mark 11:24, Jesus said it this way: *"Therefore I tell you, whatever you ask for in prayer, believe that you have received it, and it will be yours."*

I believe many Christian leaders do not truly understand the power of faith! Oh, there is mental understanding that it comes by hearing the Word of God, but when faith comes, what is next? Your faith will challenge you to think and dream bigger and to expect more than you are in the habit of expecting. Your faith will cause you to raise your sights beyond where you have grown comfortable setting them. Your faith will thrust you into victory! There is no way, as a believer, you should be receiving the Word of God regularly and not changing. The power of the Word of God will transform your life, increase your faith, and raise your sights to the destiny God has planned. Faith is the victory because it will not allow you to live by what you see and hear physically; that is only temporary.

Faith will not allow you to limit your life by where you are or where you have been. It is a spiritual force with the ability to arrange and change things. Faith is an every-winning, never-failing force that will always cause you to have victory!

In order for you to live victorious in this life of faith there are three things that you must do: receive the seed of faith, which is the Word of God, allow your patience to work with your faith and respond to the voice of God.

RECEIVE THE SEED OF FAITH

First receive the seed of faith, the Word of God, is going to require more than just hearing, memorizing or reading the Bible; you must accept and believe it as truth. God's Word will not have any more of an effect in your life if you hear it but never put it to work than if you have flower seeds in your pocket expecting them to grow. In his first letter to the church at Thessalonica, the Apostle Paul wrote, *"And we also thank God continually because, when you received the word of God, which you heard from us, you accepted it not as a human word, but as it actually is, the word of God, which is indeed at work in you who believe"* (1 Thessalonians 2:13). To see your faith obtain the victory, you must believe the Word.

ALLOW PATIENCE TO WORK

Second, you must allow your patience to work with your faith. The writer in Hebrews 6:12 clearly reveals: *"We do not want you to become lazy, but to imitate those who through faith and patience inherit what has been promised."* It is your patience that will cause you to wait on the promises of God instead of going out to make your own way. God's time is perfect time. Nothing good will ever come of running in front of God; it is through faith and patience that we will obtain the promises of God. The Greek translation for the word "patience" used here means endurance, constancy, steadfastness, and perseverance.[8] "How long should I wait, Pastor?" Until you see the object of your faith manifest is my answer!

RESPOND TO THE VOICE OF GOD

Finally, in order for faith to secure your victory, you must respond to the voice of God. Of course, to respond you must hear and know His voice. In Acts 9, you see that Saul, a persecutor of Christians, heard the voice of the Lord on the road to Damascus, and his life was changed forever. Do you notice that others with him saw a light but did not hear the voice? God's message was specifically for Paul. Being able to clearly hear God's voice is critical to you being able to do great exploits in the Kingdom of God. How will you know when to move and where to move, what to say and what to do, if you do not follow His Word? You may be able to hear the Word of God, read through verses of Scripture, but are you able to hear God's voice? If you want the victory that your faith is positioned to obtain, only take action after you have heard from God; a good move at the wrong time becomes a bad move.

Faith is the victory for all believers! It is God's desire that you triumph in all areas! Remember you are a world overcomer—your faith is your access to the power of God. It is your faith that will connect you to your God-given ability to get God ordained results, and that is your victory!

Think About It

1. As you live by faith, when trouble comes, raise your sights.

2. Your faith walk is not just for you, others are watching and learning. What are you teaching?

3. Your challenged faith will stretch you and cause you to grow up in faith.

4. A good move at the wrong time is no longer a good move.

Personal Notes

CHAPTER 5

The Just Live by Faith

"Behold the proud, His soul is not upright in him; But the just shall live by his faith." Habakkuk 2:4 (NKJV)

Right up front, before you read another word, you have to settle something that is vital to you living the victorious life of faith. So do not "speed read" the next few lines; they are going to explain a fundamental truth that God really wants His people to grasp.

YOU ARE THE RIGHTEOUSNESS OF GOD

Let that sink in before I go on to explain. **You are the righteousness of God**. Right now, out loud I want you to say, "I am the righteousness of God." Now see right there, some of you do not really believe what you just said; in fact, some of you did not even bother to repeat the sentence. Instead you allowed a gigantic flood of memories to rush in reminding you of everything you have done wrong, bringing up what you believe is your lack and shortcomings. Do you understand that is right where the enemy wants to keep you—thinking your decisions and behaviors, your lack or plenty can prevent you from becoming or keep you as the righteousness of God? Let me tell you, there is only one decision that you can make that will keep you from becoming God's righteousness, and that is the decision to accept Christ as Savior; once that decision has been made, Christ is in charge and He begins to take over.

I am not making this up. Look at the Scriptures: *"God made Him who had no sin to be sin for us, so that in Him we might become the righteousness of God"* (2 Corinthians 5:21). The "Him" Paul is speaking of here is Jesus. Jesus Christ was sinless, but became sin for you and I, so we could become the righteousness of God. It was a trade where we gave up a bag of trash and in exchange God, through Christ's finished work on Calvary offers each of us a priceless bag of treasure. Do you see that? There is absolutely nothing that you can do to earn the righteousness of God, and therefore it cannot be "unearned." Let that sink in! That is good news right there!

Now, with that understanding we can move forward. As the righteousness of God, how are you supposed to live? Let's look to the Source again: *"For therein is the righteousness of God revealed from faith to faith: as it is written, The just shall live by faith"* (Romans 1:17). This statement of truth, *"The just shall live by faith,"* is repeated four times in the Bible—Habakkuk 2:4, Romans 1:17, Galatians 3:11, and Hebrews 10:38. It seems God wants to make sure the Body of Christ gets this. Who are the "just," and what does that word mean? Simply stated, the "just" is the declared righteous. Interestingly enough, that word is derived from the same word that we find in 2 Corinthians 5:21 that is translated as "righteousness."[9] My brother and my sister, you are the just! You are the righteousness of God, declared so by Him!

"So what you are saying, Pastor, is **I** am the righteousness of God; **I** am declared just? Both of these Scriptures are talking about you and **I**?" That is correct; the Bible is talking about followers of Jesus Christ in both cases! Now I know to really receive and hold on to that, many of you are going to have to wrestle the traditional thinking and incorrect truths that have set up in your heart. I encourage you to wrestle and tear down those thoughts and any other thought that is contrary to God's Word; your thinker is vital to your doer. To live and enjoy life as God desires, to become all that He has predestined you to become, you must accept, grab hold of, and never let go of what God declares. In that accepting, you must also reject everything that is contrary to the infallible truth of God's Word.

LIVING BY FAITH

Now that you are grasping on to who you are, you can receive how God has called you to live. It is right there in the same verse: "by faith." God has called you to live by faith. In Chapter 2, the definition of faith was discussed in detail, but I want to reiterate it here. Faith is simply believing and acting on what God says. Faith is not a subject or a movement. Faith is a life that believers are to live. Faith is not a word to be used to manipulate God to do what you want, but it is what you use to access what God's grace has already secured for you. Faith believes beyond what the physical eyes see and trust in the truth of what God declares. Faith is now, faith is real, faith is power, and faith is how you, the just, the declared righteous, are to live.

I have heard people say, "I do not have that kind of faith." Now that is just not true. God dealt (imparted, bestowed) to every person THE measure of faith (Romans 12:3). I have a few questions for you to answer for yourself about that passage of Scripture. First of all, what tense is that word "dealt"? If you said "past tense," you are correct. Now for my second question, are you a part of "every person" mentioned there? If you answered yes, you are correct again. Okay, one more question. If God dealt (past tense) every person (that includes you) the measure (degree or portion) of faith, then is it possible for any believer to not have faith? If you answered no, then you are correct again! Every believer has faith; God deposited the same measure of faith inside of me that He gave to you. I submit to you that while we all have faith, we have not all developed our faith.

One day I had a young man in our ministry stand up next to me while I was preaching. I call this son TP, Total Package; he is a weight lifter. No matter how I tried to flex my biceps and triceps, they just would not stand up to TP's muscles, who by the way was not flexing, just standing there watching me. He did not have more muscles than me; no he just exercised his muscles. He did not have to flex to show what he had. The same thing is true with us in our faith. As we build our faith, we will not have to flex our "faith," it will just be obvious that we have it. The more you exercise your faith, the stronger you will grow in your faith and the more effortlessly you will live by faith. When you first started out, it took faith to believe God to heal a headache; now you believe Him to heal cancer! Do you see that? That is what happens when you live by faith.

The measure of faith you were given when you received Jesus as Lord was enough to cause you to become born again, and it is enough to bring victory over anything the world can throw at you. Go back and reread 1 John 5:4–5 from the Message Bible if you need to be encouraged in this fact. When you made Jesus Christ the Lord of your life, the faith of God took up residence in your heart. It is a gift from God. Ephesians 2:8–9 states, *"For it is by grace you have been saved, through faith—and this is not from yourselves, it is the gift of God—not by works, so that no one can boast."* Everything in the verse is a gift from God: grace, salvation, and faith. You have the faith, but you must build your faith; that is your responsibility.

BUILDING YOUR FAITH

How do you build your faith? The Word never changes; circumstances and situations change, people change, you and I change, but the Word of God never changes, it endures forever. So I keep building my faith in God's Word. Did you notice I said "keep building"? It is a never-ending process, and no matter how long you have been serving God, there is more to come, more faith to grow. Faith is present within you. It is yours to be used and developed in your daily life. God has given you this powerful faith, and it will sustain you through His Word in your faith.

To live by faith is going to take more than hoping and copying what someone else does. In every situation, you must look with the eyes of faith. That simply means look at things through God's Word. Do not be moved or shaken by what your natural eyes see or your natural ears hear. Several years ago, the doctors gave me a very negative report; I mean they had a long list of things that they were medically predicting would happen to me. I heard their diagnosis, but I chose to hear the truth of what God said to me over their medical predictions. I had to choose to live by faith, and because I had built my faith up in the Word of God, it was strong enough to carry me through that season. The time to decide to trust God and live by faith in Him and His Word is not in the middle of a crisis; as a believer you must learn to feed our spirit with the Word of God consistently; then when you are challenged, you will have what it takes to stand. Do not allow yourself to become frustrated by external occurrences. He is not taken off guard by situations. Trust God, His plan will always triumph over the enemy's plot. Jesus is the Author and Finisher of your faith,[10] and this faith has the power to make all things possible to believers!

I have learned that understanding and embracing the concept of being the just or the righteousness of God and living by faith based on that truth is a lesson that I am continually learning. Take for example, just 2.5 years ago, God told me it was time to open our second location AND He said not to take any financial resources from the main campus to do it. God told me He would provide all the finances that would be needed to open and expand His ministry. Well, I had to live by faith taking God at His Word. On one hand, I could see the finances we needed were available through the main campus, but I continued to remember God said do not touch that, trust Me. To keep the funds separated, I had the finance department to establish separate accounts internally and externally. I know to them that may have seemed extreme, but I knew what God said, and I was determined to obey Him. I will tell you the growth has been so incredible! Not only did we have to move to a larger location within a year but are in the process of expanding the new location! At every turn God has been faithful to His WORD! Praise the name of God! Faith and obedience are a powerful couple.

Living by faith is the master key that opens every door. Let me show you how vital living by faith is to believers. *"But without faith it is impossible to please him: for he that cometh to God must believe that he is, and that he is a rewarder of them that diligently seek him"* (Hebrews 11:6, KJV). Without faith, the Bible says it is <u>impossible</u> to please God; living by faith is not an option for believers. The great news is that God has called you to live by faith and He gives you the Holy Spirit to help you to accomplish all things.

God's plan for your life: *"The just shall live by faith."*[11]

Think About It

1. You are the righteousness of God.

2. God has called you to live by faith.

3. God has given you THE measure of faith; it is up to you to build on what you have been given.

4. For every believer there are only two options, live by faith, which is obedience; or live in fear, doubt, and uncertainty, which is disobedience. The choice is yours.

Personal Notes

CHAPTER 6

The Unbeatable Spirit of Faith

"I have told you these things, so that in Me you may have [perfect] peace and confidence. In the world you have tribulation and trials and distress and frustration; but be of good cheer [take courage; be confident, certain, undaunted]! For I have overcome the world. [I have deprived it of power to harm you and have conquered it for you.]" John 16:33 (AMPC)

Unbeatable is defined as "incapable of being beaten; impossible to defeat."[12] As a believer, when you are truly living your life in the spirit of faith, you are unbeatable. No matter how difficult a situation, God can turn it around. Now let that sink in real deep. Regardless if there is a trial in your health, lack in your bank account, frustrations in your family, or distress on your job, the enemy has never devised a plot that God's plan will not triumph over—God -Can -Fix -It. Do not let the devil fool you, even in times when it seems the whole world is in trouble, God can and desires to bring you through in victory.

THE VICTORY OF FATIH

Do you remember in Exodus 10, when the Egyptians were covered with darkness so thick they could not see each other moving for three days? At the same time, all the children of Israel had light in their dwellings (see verse 23). Think about that! If you will dare to believe God's Word, you can have light in the middle of a dark world, protection in the middle of a dangerous world, health in the middle of a sick world, and prosperity in the middle of an

34

impoverished world. However, let me say this: you cannot have any of that by dragging around in an attitude of defeat. If you want to walk in constant victory, you must develop an unbeatable spirit of faith.

People with an unbeatable spirit of faith always receive the blessings of God. Be careful right there, that is an easy place for you to slip into doubt as you begin to equate "always receive the blessings of God" with a life absolutely free of trials and difficulties; that is unrealistic and contrary to the Word. Everyone will go through tests and trials, but the people who have cultivated an unbeatable spirit of faith will come out supernaturally victorious every time; and while they are in the midst of troubling situations, there will be peace beyond understanding. People with an unbeatable spirit of faith have fully embraced the words Jesus spoke in John 16:33: *"I have told you these things, so that in Me you may have [perfect] peace and confidence. In the world you have tribulation and trials and distress and frustration; but be of good cheer [take courage; be confident, certain, undaunted]! For I have overcome the world. [I have deprived it of power to harm you and have conquered it for you.]"* (AMPC).

CULTIVATING THE UNBEATABLE SPIRIT OF FAITH

Paul gives a powerful insight as he describes how to cultivate that spirit in 2 Corinthians 4:13 and 18: *"We having the same spirit of faith, according as it is written, I believed, and therefore have I spoken; we also believe, and therefore speak." "While we look not at the things which are seen, but at the things which are not seen: for the things which are seen are temporal; but the things which are not seen are eternal"* (KJV). Let's look closer at those verses.

BELIEVE

The first and most fundamental fact these verses reveal about an unbeatable spirit of faith is that it believes. What does it believe? The Word of God. Faith believes God's Word just because God said it; this type of "bulldog" faith does not factor in natural circumstances. If you want to cultivate and maintain an unbeatable spirit of faith in the area of healing or finances, for example, you must stand flatfooted and undaunted contrary to what your natural eyes see, while at the same time submitting yourself to what the Word of God says. Here is the "catch," to trust and rely in what God says, you must know what God says. In other words, you must start by getting into your Bible and finding out what God said about those areas. Hearing good preaching is good, but when you take those notes home and begin to study the Word for yourself, your faith will become unbeatable. Once you have what God says on a subject you must choose to receive that Word as the truth; studying will enable you to take delivery of all that God has planned!

Of course, I am not saying you should ignore trials and distressful times, or close your eyes to them as if they are not real. They are real but according to the Scriptures, they are only temporal; that means subject to change! You can be assured that as you keep studying and standing in faith on the Word of God, those temporary situations will change!

SPEAK

In this process of spending time in the Word, keep it in your heart day after day; meditating on the promises you study. As you continue to meditate, you will begin to speak what the Word says, not what you see. Speaking is the next point we see from 2 Corinthians 4:13 and 18. Speaking is so critical in building your faith. There is natural power in words, but when you speak the Word of God you put super on that natural! You talk all the time, why not use your words to say what God says? When faced with a challenge, you must cultivate a habit of immediately speaking what God says; this will cause faith to rise up within you and situations to line up with the Word. This concept is essential in cultivating the unbeatable spirit of faith. As you speak God's word, continually remind yourself of what God decrees in Isaiah 55:11: "*so is my word that goes out my mouth: It will not return to me empty, but will accomplish what I desire and achieve the purpose for which I sent it.*"

The Bible says, you believe, therefore you speak. To change your circumstances, you must have faith in two places; in your heart and in your mouth. That is why God changed Abram's name to Abraham. Abraham means "father of many nations." Every time Abraham introduced himself after his name was changed, he was actually saying, "Hi, I'm the father of many nations." Remember, in the natural at first, he was not even the father of one. Was he lying? Absolutely not. He was simply following the example of God Himself in Romans 4:17: "*calleth those things which be not as though they were.*" You see it throughout Genesis 1:2–31. It is what you say, continually, that settles in your heart and comes to pass in your life.

Think about it, when God told Abraham that he and Sarah were going to have a baby, he took God at His Word. He was one hundred, and she was a barren ninety years old. Abraham believed and embraced the promise of God; he accepted the challenge and not the consideration. Most would be overwhelmed by those challenges, not Abraham. He believed God, and it was counted unto him for righteousness (Romans 4:3). Abraham believed God's promise, even though it seemed impossible in the natural realm. That is what the unbeatable spirit of faith does; it stands squarely in the midst of seemingly the most impossible circumstances and believes God anyway! Then it begins to speak. Choosing words carefully since faith ONLY speaks the Word of God.

FOCUSED FOCUS

The last nugget I want to pull out of 2 Corinthians 4:13 and 18 is keep your focus on what is eternal and not temporary. When developing or sustaining an unbeatable spirit of faith, keep your eyes on the Word; it is the one thing that is eternal. You cannot keep your focus on the situation and circumstance and expect to obtain the victory. Victory requires your focus and attention to be squarely on the promises of God. Keep His Word in front of your eyes and resounding in your ears while maintaining your fixed focus until you can see what your faith is grasping come to pass with the eyes of your spirit. That is what the unbeatable spirit of faith does; it looks *"not at the things which are seen, but at the things which are not seen: for the things which are seen are temporal; but the things which are not seen are eternal."*

I have said it before, and I will continue to say it; God gives us the foundation to build on. Romans 12:3 makes that point clear: *"God hath dealt to every man the measure of faith."* That Scripture was written to born again believers, therefore you can be assured that since the moment you made Jesus the Lord of your life, you have faith within you. However, also at that moment it became your responsibility to begin building on the faith God has given. The more you hear the Word, the more it will develop and grow within you. *"So then faith cometh by hearing, and hearing by the Word of God"* (Roman 10:17, KJV).

It is the unbeatable spirit of faith that reaches into the realm of the spirit, grasps the promise of God and brings forth a tangible, physical fulfillment of that promise. Sometimes I think about my own life, a little boy from Slocomb, Alabama, who went into the U.S. Army; by the world's standards, I did not have much. I remember when I knelt beside my couch at thirty-six years old and responded yes to God's call to come to Augusta, Georgia to pastor, I had no idea what was in front of me, but my faith in Him caused me to boldly say yes. I recall pulling up to a wooded area on Willis Foreman Road in Hephzibah, Georgia, and God told me to stop looking with my natural eyes, but look with His eyes at the city that He planned. When I think about how we left the house, moved to the school, marched from the school to possess the land! When I give thought to how God has taught me about the unbeatable spirit of faith, I get overwhelmed by His presence, and I am even more determined to stay in the fight, the good fight of faith—the fight that has already been won!

Proverbs 24:10 lets you know that if you faint, give up, quit in the day of adversity, trials, troubles, and discouragements, your faith is small! You cannot have small faith and an unbeatable spirit of faith at the same time. I am determined to accomplish and obtain everything that God has for me to obtain and accomplish—I am determined to live in victory with an unbeatable spirit of faith! What about you?

Think About It

1. People with an unbeatable spirit of faith believe the Word of God, speak the Word of God, and keep their focus on the Word of God.

2. You are responsible for developing an unbeatable spirit of faith within yourself.

3. Small faith, faith that quits and gives up, will render results that discourage and frustrate.

4. Even when the promise of God seems impossible believe God anyway.

Personal Notes

CHAPTER 7

More Precious Than Gold

"These have come so that the proven genuineness of your faith—of greater worth than gold, which perishes even though refined by fire—may result in praise, glory and honor when Jesus Christ is revealed." 1Peter 1:7

T oday, gold is perhaps one of the greatest commodities in this country; its value exceeding beyond paper currency. Think about it, the value of paper currency is subject to the constraints of inflation, gold is gold, and it will always be gold. However, the Word of God says that *"So that [the genuineness] of your faith may be tested, [your faith] which is infinitely more precious than the perishable gold which is tested and purified by fire"* (1 Peter 1:7, AMPC).

GENUINE FAITH

Notice in the referenced Scripture, the writer does not discuss "faith" but "genuineness of faith" or genuine faith. Before we move forward, let's look at that word "genuine." According to Merriam Webster Dictionary, something or someone who is genuine is free from pretense or hypocrisy, authentic, sincere, and real; not fake, counterfeit or false.[13] The word "genuine" is synonymous with "trustworthy," "legitimate," and "unadulterated." According to Paul, this is the type of faith that his spiritual son Timothy possessed (2 Timothy 1:5). Now, this may not be your favorite paragraph in the book, but I have to tell you, the true genuineness of your faith will never be authenticated until it is tested. That is why you are not to think it is strange or begin to question God, His Word, and His instructions when the test comes. 1 Peter 4:12 in the Amplified Bible makes that truth clear: *"Beloved, do not be surprised at the fiery ordeal which is taking place to test you [that is, to test the quality of your faith], as though something strange or unusual were happening to you."* The "fiery ordeal" is occurring to test or try or even prove the "quality of your faith."

There will be times that living this life of faith is challenging. To continue to stand on promises and move forward in the purpose, you must commit over and over again to persevere; maintaining your purpose despite the difficulties before you. As you are processing through challenging times, there will be moments when you feel alone. During those times, maintain your focus on the promise, move forward with a steady determination, and keep going regardless of the temptation to slow down or give up. It is in these times the truth of your genuine faith will be revealed.

Your faith is more precious than natural gold, because faith is the currency of the Kingdom of God. Just as the goldsmith tests gold to determine if it is pure gold or imitation, so the trials of life will test your faith to prove its genuineness. In life you cannot truly trust what you cannot test; that includes faith. Job 23:10 says, *"But He knows the way that I take; When He has tested me, I shall come forth as gold."*

TESTED FAITH

Several years ago, one of our members had an aneurysm. When I received the call, I was told the doctors said she only had a 15 percent chance of surviving. By the time I reached the hospital, she had suffered another, and because of swelling on the brain, had been placed in a medically induced coma. I shared with the doctor, "You do your part and we are going to trust God to do His part." I knew this family and knew they had an unbeatable spirit of faith. I sat down with the family and encouraged them to stay in faith and to not allow the medical prognosis to alter their faith and confidence in God and His Word. After all, gold is tried in fire to produce purity and such is the same in life and faith. This precious warrior stayed in a comma for just under three months. Today, years later, God has completely restored her! She is healthy with complete mobility; she is driving and living life as she had before. Well, life as before with one exception; they are living with an amazing testimony of the victorious life of faith! The genuineness of their faith has been tested, placed in the heat of trials and come forth pure and more precious than gold!

On occasion, every one of you will encounter tests and trials and when they come, it may be easy to get discouraged. Discouragement is a feeling and God knows you have feelings; He gave them to you. However, even in the midst of <u>challenges</u> and <u>adversity</u>, God expects His children to respond in line with what He has taught through His Word.

THE RIGHT RESPONSE

What does a right response look like? To answer that question let's look at a verse from the book of James. James 1:2–4 instructs us to *"Consider it wholly joyful, my brethren, whenever you are enveloped in or encounter trials of any sort or fall into various temptations. Be assured and understand that the trial and proving of your faith bring out endurance and steadfastness and patience. But let endurance and steadfastness and patience have full play and do a thorough work, so that you may be [people] perfectly and fully developed [with no defects], lacking in nothing."* (AMPC) The Word of God teaches to rejoice during difficulty. Of course this does not mean that you are to be glad about the hardship. However, you can be joyful in the midst of trouble because you know that God, who loves you and is in complete control, is using the circumstances to prepare and grow you in His Word and will. Even though having a positive attitude during a difficult and challenging time seems illogical, it is possible, and it is God's desired response from His children. Let me share a few reasons to explain this point.

ENDURANCE

First of all, God uses difficult experiences, to instruct you in endurance. Often, your natural reaction to difficulty and pain is to run away as quickly as possible. However, God wants you to "hang in there" so you can glean the full benefit of whatever lesson He has for you. Right here I need to say that God does not put things on you or orchestrate difficult and painful situations in your life; that is not the God we serve. However, He will use situations that you encounter to strengthen you and bring glory to His name!

PURIFY

Second, your heavenly Father uses tests and trials as a refining fire to separate His children from what is toxic in their lives which will lead them into greater spiritual maturity. He has a plan for each believer and struggles are one of the tools He uses to prepare us to do His will. In the process of difficulty, you will find that your faith has been strengthened. Remember the example of the muscle builder. He is continually strengthened and developed as carefully weight and resistance is applied.

PROVEN

Third, it is in the heat of adversity that the genuineness of your faith in God is proven, just as gold when it is refined and purified in fire to determine and demonstrated its authenticity. When you begin to understand that God makes positive use of your adversities, you will become more confident in facing them, trusting He always has your best interest in mind. This leads to joy, because you know He is building your endurance, purifying your hearts, and shaping you into a person with unshakeable trust in Him.

One of the most precious things that you possess as a believer is your faith; you are saved by grace through it, healed by it, live by it, walk by it, justified by it, made righteous by it, and obtain victory through it. Your faith is so precious and vital that without it you are not able to please God. It is through faith that God is pleased, and you are able to obtain a good report. It is through your faith that God and others see how much we truly trust God. Brothers and sisters, your genuine faith is priceless!

Often when people face challenging situations, painful moments and trials, the all-time favorite question is asked: "Why me, God?" Some will even lay out to God a list of "accomplishments" as if how well you perform will prevent life from occurring or difficulty from coming your way. I want to encourage you, continue to stand firm; trust and believe that God's plan is perfect, and as you continue in obedience, the genuineness of your faith will be revealed. Yes, it is going to call for you to stretch, but wait, I am getting ahead of myself. Trust God, stand firm, and know that the genuineness of your faith is more precious than gold.

Think About It

1. Do not be surprised when your faith is tested.

2. When challenges come it is your advance preparation that will determine your reaction—faith or fear.

3. God does not "put bad things on you" nor does He create disaster, but He will use these trials to strengthen your faith, if you allow Him to do so.

4. God loves you!

Personal Notes

CHAPTER 8

Stretching Your Faith

*"Nor do we boast and claim credit for the work someone else
has done. Instead, we hope that your faith will grow so that
the boundaries of our work among you will be extended."*
2 Corinthians 10:15 (NLT)

L et me tell you right up front that my assignment for this
chapter is to challenge and encourage you to allow your
faith to be stretched beyond measure. The purpose of
my assignment is not just for your personal benefit but for the
assignment God has on your life—to enlarge the Kingdom of God.
It is a personal stretch with global impact potential.

Allow me to share with you the end of this chapter at the
beginning. As your faith is stretched or increased you can expect at
least five very powerful things to happen in your immediate circle.

5 INEVITABLE EFFECTS OF THE STRETCH

- Stronger families, marriages, and children as wisdom is lived
  out.
- Greater unity, fire, passion, and servanthood within your local
  church.
- More members of the Body of Christ challenged to step out
  and allow their own faith to be stretched.
- Transformation of communities thereby causing a greater
  impact in the cities.
- More lost souls reached for the Kingdom of God.

I know each of those occurrences is important to you, otherwise, you would have laid this book down before you finished the introduction. I shared the sweetness of victory in allowing your faith to be stretched up front because it will make my next statement easier to accept. Faith stretching will not always be comfortable, it will not always be easy. In fact, often times the stretch will be a struggle, riddled with uncertainty, discomfort, and yes, even pain.

I do not want to sound discouraging; my intent is to present you with truth in hopes that you will keep the victory before you while you are enduring the stretch. That concept is no different than what Christ did for you. Look at Hebrews 12:2: *"For the joy set before him he endured the cross, scorning its shame, and sat down at the right hand of the throne of God."* The "joy" being spoken of here is you and I. He looked past the cross to the joy on the other side. Well, when you are in the midst of your stretch you have look for the fruit, victory and joy on the other side that God has planned for others as well as you. Keeping this focus will strengthen you and enable you to successfully push past the desire to give up.

CONTINUOUS STRETCH

The word stretch means to go beyond or to increase. Think back five or ten years ago or even last year. Do you remember the faith struggles you had back then? Do you remember the things your faith had to wrestle, the unbelief that continued to try to take you over? How did you get from there to where you are right now in your faith? I am glad you asked. You allowed God to stretch your faith and to grow you up in areas! God continuously looks to keep your faith active. Active faith is growing faith . . . stagnate faith is dead. God takes you from faith to faith, from glory to glory causing you to believe Him for more . . . for greater. Now I am not just talking about finances, look at the list again: stronger families, greater unity, increase in the harvest of souls, transformation—God is bigger than a bank account!

You know the Scriptures declare four times *"the just shall live by faith."* That makes it clear that "faith" is not a place you visit or vacation yearly or when the situation mandates. Faith is a place you live, a place you grow from. God has given each of you the measure of faith, but it is up to each of person, individually, to allow that faith to be stretched so that it will mature, develop and increase.

THE STRETCH IS VITAL

From the time I went into the United States Army as a private until I retired as a first sergeant, almost daily we endured some physical training. When I was a young buck, there were mornings when it was freezing cold and I would just want the run to begin, to just get started. I knew the run would warm us up, but those "wise old sergeants" would take us through a series of stretching exercises that seem to have no good purpose in the midst of the cold. When I became one of those "wise old sergeants" I learned the importance of stretching. I learned stretching helped prevent injuries, increased performance, and allowed the blood to flow freely to the muscles carrying oxygen and nutrients: in short. I learned the vital necessity of stretching. The same is so in your walk with Christ . . . in your faith walk. Stretching your faith in Christ, trusting in and submitting to Him more and more protects you from injury, increases your performance to His glory, and allows the benefits of the free flowing blood to keep you! God wants to stretch your faith daily! Yes, stretch daily and in every situation! Look at Proverbs 3:5–6 *"Trust in the Lord with all your heart, and do not lean on your own understanding. In all your ways acknowledge him and he will make straight your paths"* (ESV). When you operate in line with that Scripture, it is going to stretch your faith in a very real way—daily.

3 LESSONS FROM THE TURTLE

When I was a little boy, I was fascinated with turtles. I would watch them stick their neck and legs out to move a little, and when they were finished moving, they would draw all body parts back into the shell. When they were ready to move forward again, they would stick their neck and legs out again and begin moving forward. You know you can learn a lot from the turtle.

- First of all, you have to be ready to move before you will allow the stretching to begin. Until you are ready, you will just stay in your safe place doing what you do in your safe place—which is everything except grow. Oh, you will talk about growing, but without stretching, growth will not occur.

- Second, when you are ready to move and grow there will be action on your part. Have you ever seen someone who is waiting for Jesus to do something they should be doing themselves? I mean, they are diligently "waiting" in faith without corresponding action and then become frustrated and disgruntled when "God lets them down." What did James say in James 2:17? *"In the same way, faith by itself, if it is not accompanied by action, is dead."* You can talk faith all day long, but talking will not cause or promote a stretch or growth.

- The third lesson from the turtle is you are responsible for the action. God has given each of us the measure of faith, but growth and development of that faith . . . the process of the stretch is an individual responsibility and choice.

STRETCHING FAITH = GROWING FAITH

To stretch your faith, you must stir up your faith; ignite, inflame, kindle up, awaken your faith! Keep it blazing in flames. I am talking about faith that is so stirred up until you continuously believe in your heart and constantly confess with your mouth what God has said about a situation. I am talking about so stirred up that your Pastor has to thank God for the extraordinary growth of your faith, just as Paul did for the church at Thessalonica (2 Thessalonians 1:3). So stirred up that when situations occur, you immediately see them as opportunities for God to be glorified!

You will begin to recognize that you are growing and maturing when what others see as struggles, challenges, or mountains, you see as potential faith stretchers. Your goals and visions will stretch your faith, if they are from God, your family will stretch your faith, and your ministry will stretch your faith!

Let me say right here, please do not use others as a standard by which you measure your faith, your call, or what you hear from God. In fact, if people are attempting to talk you out of stretching your faith, listening to the whole counsel of God or compromise what God has instructed you to do, be careful of the hindrance. We may all start out on the same level according to Romans 12:3, *the same measure,* but we do not all stay at the same place. The Body of Christ is filled with people who are operating in mental assent (agreeing mentally that God's Word is true and <u>can</u> work "but") verses heart faith (being fully persuaded that God is faithful and true in every situation). You cannot stir up or stretch mental assent.

Yes, it is true allowing your faith to be stretched will be challenging, but each of us much choose in every situation to accept the challenge not the consideration. Go back to the beginning of this chapter . . . look at the five areas that you will be inviting God to enter and change if you simply submit to the stretching.

Let's close this chapter with a few words of encouragement from a man who understood being stretched for Christ. *"Brothers and sisters, I do not consider myself yet to have taken hold of it. But one thing I do: Forgetting what is behind and straining toward what is ahead, I press on toward the goal to win the prize for which God has called me heavenward in Christ Jesus. All of us, then, who are mature should take such a view of things. And if on some point you think differently, that too God will make clear to you"* (Philippians 3:13–15).

Brothers and sisters—let the stretching begin or continue!

Think About It

1. The benefits of stretched faith outweigh the struggle—do not quit!

2. Is your faith active and growing or stagnate and dead?

3. You are responsible.

4. You can only stretch and stir up faith not mental assent.

Personal Notes

CHAPTER 9

Using Your Faith on Purpose

"In the same way, faith by itself, if it is not accompanied by action, is dead. But someone will say, "You have faith; I have deeds." Show me your faith without deeds, and I will show you my faith by my deeds." James 2:17–18

E very project God has assigned to me since I have become His servant has required that I use my faith on purpose. Just like a carpenter uses a hammer and nails to build or like my beloved, Janice uses those seasonings and spices to create that holiday masterpiece; in both cases, the use is always on purpose if success is to be consistent and sure. Jesus used His faith on purpose, and as His followers, we should be mimicking that example.

RAISING THE ROOF

Let me share an account of a group of men who used their faith for someone else, on purpose. Motivated and propelled by their faith, these brave men did not consider what the crowd might think or say. It happened when Jesus was in Capernaum preaching the Word. (The Word was proclaiming The Word!) The place He was preaching in was so packed with people that no one could fit in or near the door! (That is exciting to me!) Along came some men accompanied by four men carrying a paralyzed man; that is a nice sized group. Well, now if there is no standing room in the place you know there is no place for a stretcher and the group that accompanied. What do you do? Well, I will tell you what they did not do. That group did not give up and go back home. They used their faith on purpose. They broke the rules and the roof, lowering that paralyzed man through the roof and before Jesus. Mark 2:5 says, *"When Jesus saw their faith, he said to the paralyzed man, 'Son, your sins are forgiven.'"* **Jesus saw their faith**, and He responded! Ma'am, sir, I do not know about you, but I want Jesus to see my faith in action.

To use something, you employ the thing for some purpose or put it into service. God wants you to employ or utilize your faith, on purpose or intentionally. Faith is the producer of good reports. Nothing works without it! Salvation is impossible without faith! Healing is impossible without faith! Victory cannot be obtained without faith! God wants to see people saved, healed, and living in victory. If that was not the desire of the Father, He would not have sent Jesus; that was His very purpose. God wants you to intentionally use your faith to obtain the good report that has already been secured for you.

The faith I am discussing here and throughout this book is not a movement. It is life, or I should say, a lifestyle. Your faith is your personal practical expression of your confidence in God and His Word. Let me tell you right now, if you do not have faith in God's Word, you do not have faith in God. You know the enemy wants you to fear that God will not do what He says He will do. However, people who are determined to live a faith filled life will know in their "knower" that God is faithful to the end. These are the people who refuse to let go of the promises of God. Regardless of what is going on, they still see victory, and they understand that the promise comes by faith (Romans 4:16). These are the people who use their faith on purpose, despite what it looks like or what people say, to obtain the victory that God has spoken! Are you one of "these people"? Abraham was and the Bible tells us why.

MAN OF FAITH

Despite all odds, Abraham believed God, using his faith on purpose. When it was no longer sensible to have hope, Abraham still believed. Take some time to read Romans 4 in its entirety; but for the sake of time here, I just want to share verses 18 through 21: *"Against all hope, Abraham in hope believed and so became the father of many nations, just as it had been said to him, 'So shall your offspring be.' Without weakening in his faith, he faced the fact that his body was as good as dead—since he was about a hundred years old—and that Sarah's womb was also dead. Yet he did not waver through unbelief regarding the promise of God, but was strengthened in his faith and gave glory to God, being fully persuaded that God had power to do what he had promised."* Who against *hope* believed in hope; that is a powerful statement! Hope, by itself, has no power to change your circumstances, but it is a goal setter. Hope sets the goal; but faith, when you use it, goes to secure the goal. You must have hope, you cannot live without hope. It strengthens your faith!

WEAK FAITH

King James Version says in verse 19, *"And being not weak in faith."* What is weak faith? Weak faith considers the problem, instead of the promise and the circumstances instead of the Law of Faith. Individuals who have weak faith have not matured, and in their immaturity allow, the lies of satan to dictate with a louder voice than God's Word. Using your faith on purpose will strengthen you and bring you to a place where you begin to give no credit to contrary evidence. In fact, you will begin to say "I am not considering the problems; I am only accepting the promise!" That is exactly what Abraham did when *"he considered not his own body now dead, when he was about a hundred years old, neither yet the deadness of Sarah's womb."* He looked past the natural and remained fixed on the promise God had given.

As you begin to intentionally use your faith, you will become more confident in God and His Word. Contrary to what many believe, no one just stumbles into confidence. Confidence has to be developed. It is developed in that personal time you spend with God learning that you have a covenant with God and whatever He says He will do. I am sure that confidence in his covenant inspired the little shepherd boy in 1 Samuel 17 to run boldly head-on against a giant. David had faith in his God, he knew he had a covenant with God, and he also knew that Goliath did not! David used his faith; faith that was developed while others slept, faith that was increased each time he had to defend his sheep, faith that was nurtured as he created and sang songs to God! That shepherd boy grew up to be a king using his faith in God every step of the way! Faith brings God on the scene! You can rest assured, when God steps in, opposition bows out, things change, and victory is sure.

Faith is not faith without corresponding action. You must employ, put faith to work on your behalf. "Faith" will not yield results, bringing victory in your life unless you use it intentionally; even in the face of opposition. Yes, opposition will come but you have to set yourself up and not "stagger." Romans 4:20–21 (AMP) says, *"But he did not doubt or waver in unbelief concerning the promise of God, but he grew strong and empowered by faith, giving glory to God, being fully convinced that God had the power to do what He had promised."* Other versions say he did not stagger. To stagger is to withdraw from or be separated from. Abraham did not withdraw from God's promise. He held on and remained steadfast. He disregarded contrary opinions, comments, and reports. Abraham was fully persuaded and convinced the promises of God would happen. When he refused to doubt, waiver, or stagger the result developed his faith. He became stronger and empowered by his faith!

4 STRENGTHENING PRINCIPLES

Let me share four principles that will strengthen you to use your faith in the midst of every situation.

- Begin with the Word. Search the promise of God. You have to know and understand what your faith is based on.

- Meditate on those promises until faith rises in your heart. As you study the greatness of your God and His steadfast love, you will become strengthened. As you are strengthened in your faith, your automatic response to situations will be to use your faith.

- Act on what the Word says. Just do what God says and leave the results to Him.

- Finally, consider the matter done! Give glory to God in advance!

Using your faith on purpose will render victorious living, and that is God's desire for your life!

Think About It

1. If you want to successfully live a victorious life you must learn to consistently use your faith on purpose

2. Hoping will never change your circumstances but faith will.

3. You have a covenant with God—your problems do not.

4. Your faith requires your corresponding actions.

Personal Notes

CHAPTER 10

Keep Your Faith Switch On

"Be on your guard; stand firm in the faith; be courageous; be strong." 1 Corinthians 16:13

T he Lord said to me, "Many believers have turned off their 'faith switch' because of what is going on in the world." Numerous followers of Jesus Christ are so focused on talk of recession, shut downs—even at the national government level, economic and financial crisis, and poor housing and job market, that they are losing their focus on God. Then they look at personal and relational crisis and turmoil; divorce, separation, homelessness, violence, social issues that plague the youth—and the list goes on and on! Such a bombardment of the mind with negative input that unless you set yourself that you will not be moved by what you see or hear . . . unless you dogmatically focus on God and His Word, your "faith switch" will be flipped to the off position before you realize what has occurred.

Yes, your head knows: *"We walk by faith and not by sight."*[14] However, all of the negative seeing and hearing, which not only has the potential but the purpose of taking your focus off of what God says, is hitting the target in the hearts of many. Do not be deceived; your faith is of great value to the enemy, He is fully aware that in your faith lies power because he knows that nothing is impossible to the person who believes (Mark 9:23). Further, satan knows nothing in the Kingdom of God operates apart from faith. As a matter of fact, we cannot please or satisfy God without faith (Hebrews 11:6), and your enemy is aware of that. Your enemy knows the Word of God, and he knows your victory plan. However, his knowing has no effect on the faith life of the believer if you know and follow the plan that God has laid out! To stand firm in your faith, you have to keep your faith switch on, no wavering back and forth between your circumstances and God's promises—believing one then the other. What did James say? *"But let him ask in faith, with no doubting, for the one who doubts is like a wave of the sea that is driven and tossed by the wind. For that person must not suppose that he will receive anything from the Lord; he is a double-minded man, unstable in all his ways."*[15]

SHORT CIRCUIT ALERT

I know sometimes it is easy to get into conversations or watch something that, even subtly, attacks your faith. Then after you walk away or change the channel, you begin to process what you heard or said over and over again. Watch out, this is a faith switch short circuit in the making. Think about it, what is a short circuit? When the components or connections in a circuit are damaged or connected improperly, it prevents the electricity from flowing correctly. When what you see affects what you think and what you say, it begins to damage your faith connection, and if you are not careful, will cause your faith switch to flip to off. Let me say right here, faith **always** says what God says, always. Before we move forward, let me remind you of a vital battle point. Look at 1 John 5:4 in the Amplified Bible: *"For everyone born of God is victorious and overcomes the world; and this is the victory that has conquered and overcome the world—our [continuing, persistent] faith [in Jesus the Son of God]."* Let's also look at the same passage from the Message Bible; *"Every God-begotten person conquers the world's ways. The conquering power that brings the world to its knees is our faith."* Your victory to overcome the world is wrapped up in your faith! Others around you may see the same thing you see, but you are called and prepared to respond differently. Your response should be a response filled with hope and faith in God. This is a response that will not only bring victory for you but will be a witness to others, nonbelievers and believers who are seeking to grow, who are watching you live your faith-filled life.

FAITH THAT WILL NOT QUIT

Do not fall into the trap of assuming that keeping your faith switch turned on is Holy Spirit's responsibility; no sir, no ma'am, that is the responsibility of the believer—that is your job. Think of it like this, the electric company that services your house has an obligation, once you enter into a contract, to connect electricity to your home. Beyond that point, it becomes the homeowner's responsibility how that electricity is used. When adversity, difficulties, or challenges come, you must choose to keep that switch on by keeping God and His Word as your focal point. The enemy and your flesh will do everything possible to distract you, but the decision is yours and yours alone.

You have to be like David when he faced Goliath. The warriors of Israel were focused on the size of the giant; David was focused on the size of his God! The warriors of Israel considered the strength of Goliath, but David considered the strength of his God! David knew he had a covenant with God AND he knew the uncircumcised Philistine did not. With his faith in God firmly set, he knew the head of this giant had to come off, and no one could say anything to cause him to doubt; not ridicule from his brother, doubt from the king, or taunting from the giant! David kept his faith switch on, and the end result was the giant fell, the enemies were defeated and hope was restored![16] If the Body of Christ would only grab hold of the power of faith—; UNWAIVERING, RELENTLESS, CONSISTENT FAITH, the world would see the effects everywhere and in every situation!

You see the same unyielding faith in the life of Abraham as he too ignored the natural evidence around him and believed God's promises! Just as Abraham chose to ignore the obvious aging of his body, as well as Sarah's—just as David chose to give no consideration to the size of the giant—every believer must choose to consider God over every contrary situation. Somewhere along the way both of these men decided to turn on their faith switch, and keep it on. They made irreversible decisions to go with God, and then stepped past the point of no return. If you and I are ever going to see God do the impossible in our lives . . . in our situations . . . in our family . . . in our ministry . . . in our neighborhoods, cities, nation, or world, we are going to have to do the same thing. Keep your faith switch on!

"BUT HOW?"

"How," you ask, "how do you keep the faith switch on?" It is the same answer; it is in the Word of God. Search the promises of God, and believe what He has said and is saying about your need. Meditate on God's promises until faith rises in your heart. The word meditate does not indicate a passing thought. It means to think deeply and carefully. As a county boy, it makes me think of an old cow that chews on their cud for a long time just getting everything out of what they are chewing. That needs to be how you treat the Word of God. In that meditation process, remember faith comes by hearing the Word of God.[17] Speak the Word that you are studying and meditating on; hearing that Word will cause your faith in God and His Word to rise up quickly! Speaking out God's Words releases God's ability on your behalf. You also need to act on what the Word says. There is no way to keep your faith switch on if you do not consistently do what God says do. Inconsistent actions and behavior renders inconsistent results. Finally, consider the matter done, giving glory to God in advance. Your faith is a practical expression of your confidence in God and in His Word. Belief starts it and faith carries it out! At this point, praise Him in advance for the victory!

With your faith switch securely locked in the on position, taking action will be an easier step, but that is the next chapter.

Think About It

1. Your enemy, satan is defeated but not ignorant—be alert at all times.

2. Faith always says what the Word of God says. If you are saying different, check your faith switch.

3. You must make an irreversible decision before the giants appear.

4. If you obey the Word of God sometimes and believe the Word of God sometimes, is it logical to expect to receive God's best all of the time? Consistency is paramount.

Personal Notes

CHAPTER 11

Faith's Corresponding Action

"So also faith, if it does not have works (deeds and actions of obedience to back it up), by itself is destitute of power (inoperative, dead)." James 2:17 (AMPC)

Y ou know faith is a spiritual force that works in the life of every born again believer, and it is set in motion by believing and acting on the Word of God. Faith is the producer of all victories and good reports in your life. Nothing happens by coincidence or happenstance. There is a vital truth you have to learn, understand, and apply; to effectively operate in the Kingdom of God, you must learn to live by faith. The more you learn the lesson of faith, the more successful you will be in your faith living.

STUCK IN HOPE

Here is the problem with many believers—they believe and speak faith but get stuck in hope. Since you cannot fully act on what you do not comprehend, let me help you right now to understand the difference in faith and hope. It is very simple, hope is always future tense—looking forward, pointing to the future, anticipating some potential occurrence. Faith, on the other hand is now; faith says I have it right now. Faith says, "I am not in a mode of anticipating but I am in a mode of celebrating because I have already received what my faith has secured for me."

Let's look at a very familiar passage of scripture to further explain. Now listen, do not run past this verse because you are able to quote it in six Bible versions and three languages. A word of sound advice; every time you touch or come in contact with God's Word, it should be like the first time. There is ALWAYS something new to glean from Scripture. The day you stop receiving from God's Word, the day you feel you cannot learn more from every Scripture, is a day you are in a very dangerous place.

Having said that, let's look at Hebrews 11:1 (AMPC): "*Now faith is the assurance (the confirmation, the title deed) of the things [we] hope for, being the proof of things [we] do not see and the conviction of their reality [faith perceiving as real fact what is not revealed to the senses].*" Faith says you have what you were hoping for now, and in your having you begin to act on what you have; that is called corresponding action.

BEHAVING LIKE YOU ARE BELIEVING

When you are in faith, there will always be action taken to demonstrate your faith. That action might be as simple as confessing with your mouth, "Thank You, Father. I believe I have received my request now, as I pray." True faith requires and will always be accompanied by corresponding actions. Look at the Weymouth translation of James 2:14: "*What good is it, my brethren, if a man professes to have faith, and yet his actions do not correspond?*" Later, in verse 22, the Bible says of Abraham, "*You notice, that his faith was cooperating with his actions, and by his actions his faith was perfected.*" We can clearly see another example of actions that corresponds with faith in Luke 7 when Jesus was heading to the house of the centurion to heal the centurion's faithful servant. The centurion put action to his faith by sending someone to tell Jesus "*Lord, don't trouble yourself, for I do not deserve to have you come under my roof. That is why I did not even consider myself worthy to come to you. But say the word, and my servant will be healed.*" Shortly thereafter, we hear the testimony of a healed servant!

I think of my own life how by faith, phase by phase, the main campus of Faith Outreach Church has risen from what was once thirty acres of woods. With each step, with each phase, and with each new structure, we had to put action to our faith. If we would have sat wishing and hoping we would still be sitting, wishing, and hoping in the woods without a single building. Faith without corresponding actions will not work, it is just that simple. A faith-filled confession plus wrong actions will result in faith failure. One of the greatest mistakes believers make is to confess faith in the Word of God, while at the same time contradicting confessions with wrong actions. Faith without fitting action is dead! Your actions must correspond with your believing if you are going to receive from God! You cannot blame your faith failures on God if you are saying one thing and doing something else, you are only deluding yourself by being divided within yourself.

I love the book of James; it is the blueprint for the faith life. James, the half-brother of Jesus, gives very practical instruction for living a life of faith. Throughout this book, we see faith connected to doing. In James 1:22, he instructs believers to hear and DO the Word of God. You know Abraham was not justified because he said "I believe God"; Abraham acted on what he believed. Rahab, an Amorite harlot, believed if she would help God's spies they would spare her. She put action to her faith, and the end result is she will forever be listed in the *Hall of Faith*.

What is the correct corresponding action to your faith? The correct corresponding action for you is what God and His Word tells you to do. Yes, it is just that simple, and yet just that complex. There is no cookie cutter answer; however, allow me to give you a few guidelines to help you with the "acid test" in determining your God-mandated set of actions.

MEASURING CORRESPONDING ACTIONS

- Corresponding actions of faith will never contradict the Word of God. In other words, God will not have you to act on something He calls sin. Let me explain it like this, God will not tell you that your next beloved is the beloved of another. Putting actions to that is following your flesh and many will be destroyed by your attempt to spiritualize your sin. God's Word stands forever and above all.

- Corresponding actions of faith will not be lip service but lifestyle. You cannot live the life of faith part-time expecting and demanding full-time benefits.

- Corresponding actions of faith steps out. You will know that God is in the middle and directing your actions when you can say "I cannot do this." Look at how Abraham went to sacrifice his son, his promise, and look at how quickly God moved.

- Corresponding actions of faith speaks out. Your words are containers filled with power, and they will produce after their own kind. Here is the question: are your words filled with faith in God or faith in your fears?

Before I end this chapter, let's take a look at Matthew 7:24–27, Jesus said, "*These words I speak to you are not incidental additions to your life, homeowner improvements to your standard of living. They are foundational words, words to build a life on. If you work these words into your life, you are like a smart carpenter who built his house on solid rock. Rain poured down, the river flooded, a tornado hit—but nothing moved that house. It was fixed to the rock. But if you just use my words in Bible studies and don't work them into your life, you are like a stupid carpenter who built his house on the sandy beach. When a storm rolled in and the waves came up, it collapsed like a house of cards*" (MSG). When you align your doing with your believing, you will become better equipped to withstand life's storms. In the preceding verses, Jesus shares how different people react to the storms of life. When the storms of life come, some fall or buckle spiritually under pressure, in other words, they experience faith failures. The problem is these people are not doers of the Word; practicing the instruction contained within. These believers are speaking one thing and doing another—having actions that do not correspond to the professed faith. Jesus said when you hear the Word and do not do what you have heard, you are not operating in wisdom and you will fail. Faith's corresponding action is to bring about success—the success God wants and has predestined for you.

I have shown you how important it is to ensure your actions correspond with your faith, now it is time for you to be about doing what you have been shown. This is a lesson you will need as you proceed to the next chapter; a chapter whose subject matter is a struggle for so many.

Let's go forward.

Think About It

1. Hope anticipates. Faith has it now. Your actions will reveal where you are in the process.

2. Faith requires corresponding actions.

3. Your words must correspond to your faith or your results will not correspond to your desires.

4. In considering actions to correspond with your faith remember—obey the Word of God.

Personal Notes

CHAPTER 12

Faith Works by Love

"For [if we are] in Christ Jesus, neither circumcision nor uncircumcision counts for anything, but only faith activated and energized and expressed and working through love."
Galatians 5:6 (AMPC)

I f you are going to live a victorious life that is pleasing to God, you are going to have to live by faith. In living by faith, it cannot be segregated living. Segregated living is where you separate your life; in one pile is your "live by faith" stack and the other pile is your "live by flesh" stack. Consistent victorious living will only come by consistently living by faith, in all areas of your life. I believe the most important aspect of Christian living a believer must embrace after salvation is faith. In truth, this concept of Godly faith is so deep and so broad that we will never exhaust the fullness of God's meaning. However, as a believer, disciple of Christ, it should be your desire to try. It is your faith that pleases God, and I am confident that is a goal you and I have in common.

GOD'S KIND OF LOVE

Through more than twenty years of pastoring, I have discovered that one of the areas many believers struggle in is love; accepting and receiving God's love, loving others, and loving themselves as God commands. The God kind of love is without condition, regardless of wrongs committed, differences, or reciprocation; God commands you to love EVERYONE. Now, I am not telling you that is an easy task. As a matter of fact, sometimes it is extremely difficult. However, let me say, it is possible in every situation. I know that is truth because if it were not God would not have given the command to love everyone. "Okay, Pastor, what does that have to do with faith?" My answer to that question is love has everything to do with faith. God's goal for this chapter is to reveal that truth to you in such a profound way that your love and faith walk will be strengthened and energized.

FAITH-LOVE CONNECTION

Faith is filtered through love; it is activated, energized, expressed, and worked through love. Love inspires faith. It gives faith a foundation to build on and gives you reason to believe.

Think about the love of God or the love God has for you. His unquestionable limitless love for you is the foundation of your faith in Him. John 3:16 (KJV) says, *"For God so loved the world, that he gave his only begotten Son, that whosoever believeth in him should not perish, but have everlasting life."* Do you see that? I get so excited when I think about God's love for me, God's love for you. It was God's love that drew and continues to draw me. The more I learn about God's love, the more I know I can trust Him; I know I can place my full and complete confidence in Him. Think about it, what is confidence? Confidence is defined as full trust and belief in the ability of someone or something.[18] Okay, then what is faith? Faith is believing and acting on God's Word; it is a practical expression of the confidence you have in God and His Word. How did that confidence begin, and how does that faith start and continue to grow? Simple, it is through God's unconditional love. Do you see that connection between love and faith? I have said it before and I will say it over and over again—nothing, absolutely nothing in the Kingdom of God operates apart from faith. The power of faith has the potential of reaching and affecting every area of your life!

Until you discover who you are in Christ and how much God loves you, your faith will not work as it is designed. In other words, you will always question what the Word says about you; doubting whether God will do what He said, questioning His love for you, fretful and fearful of the future. The Word of God says in 1 John 4:17–18 (KJV), *"Herein is our love made perfect, that we may have boldness in the day of judgment: because as he is, so are we in this world. There is no fear in love; but perfect love casteth out fear: because fear hath torment. He that feareth is not made perfect in love."* Your faith, activated, energized, expressed, and working through love, will cast out fear and doubt.

GOD LOVES YOU

Faith works by love, when you have faith in Love (God). As a believer, you must have faith in the fact that God loves you; you must fully trust that unchangeable fact. You see, religion expressed through religious teachings, traditions, and mindsets have messed so many people up. People are in the church thinking they must qualify for the love of God. People are standing outside the church thinking they must qualify for the love of God. Both groups are wounded, desperate to find truth in the midst of chaos, thinking that they must qualify for the love of God. So many walking around <u>feeling</u> and <u>saying</u>, "I am not worthy." As a Pastor, it grieves my heart.

Yes, it is true, in yourself you are not worthy, none are; but you are not in yourself, you are in Christ. In Christ is where your true worth and value are found. Listen, until you accept and receive the fullness of God's love you will never truly be able to love others or yourself as He requires. That deficiency affects your faith since faith works by love. Love is the force behind faith. It is explosive and active; it causes great things to happen.

FAITH AND LOVE IN ACTION

Faith works by love. If you are not walking in love, your faith will be blocked from producing. Faith will not work apart from love. Look at 1 Corinthians 13:2: *"If I have the gift of prophecy and can fathom all mysteries and all knowledge, and if I have a faith that can move mountains, but do not have love, I am nothing."* Faith to move mountains without love is profitless. You must choose to live your life operating in love even when love is not returned. I remember once when I was in a business venture and one of the ladies involved was so rude, I mean she was just mean. It was unprovoked and unwarranted, but it was direct. Well I chose to walk in love so that my faith would not be hindered, and I chose to express my love by sending her some flowers. Now I do not know what that did for her, but for me, I was free and my faith was activated and energized. I will just say that God was successful in that business venture.

Let's try a little exercise. Right now declare, out loud, "I am God's beloved! I am not going to be loved by Him; I am already loved by Him. Since I am assured of His love for me I can love myself and others without condition. My faith will not be hindered because I choose to walk according to the Word of God and that is by faith and in love. I have God's faith and God's love on the inside of me and I use it in every situation to bring Him glory." Receive that in Jesus' Name!

Say that a few times if you need to. Let that sink in and become a part of your thinking. In the next chapter, I am going to discuss shaping or framing your world and to a large degree, that is accomplished with your words. Just like the words we just spoke . . . God's Word, filled with faith that works by love.

Are you ready?

Think About It

1. If you are not experiencing consistent victorious living, ask yourself, "Am I consistently living by faith?" If the answer is no, adjust your living.

2. Your faith victories are directly connected to the love you have for God, others, and yourself.

3. God loves you. It is not a love you can earn so you cannot "unearn" it—receive the gift.

4. Until you truly receive and accept God's love, your faith will be crippled.

Personal Notes

CHAPTER 13

Framing Your World with Faith

"By faith we understand that the worlds [during the successive ages] were framed (fashioned, put in order, and equipped for their intended purpose) by the word of God, so that what we see was not made out of things which are visible." Hebrews 11:3 (AMPC)

Often people have big dreams and visions in life that do not manifest because there is a failure to mix the main ingredient that needs to be combined with that dream or vision. You know hope is a goal setter, but faith is the key to the manifestation of what you hope for. There will not be a shaping or framing of your world, hopes, dreams, and visions apart from <u>applied</u> faith.

Faith is the force God used to create everything you can see. Yes, it is true, by faith, God called into existence the created world, shaped, and framed by His words. *"By faith, we see the world called into existence by God's word, what we see created by what we don't see."* Hebrews 11:3 (MSG) Do you see that? By faith your God shaped and framed this world. In Ephesians 5:1 (MSG), what did the Apostle Paul instruct believers to do? *"Watch what God does, and then you do it, like children who learn proper behavior from their parents."* From these Scriptures you see that just as God used faith to frame the world, as you follow His example, you should be doing the same; shaping and framing your world by faith.

Since faith is the parent force of all that exists, the natural world will respond to faith. Everything that you can contact with the five physical senses is subject to the force of faith. One thing I am convinced of, if God could not do anything without faith, neither can you or I. How did God frame the world? It was through His spoken words; words filled with faith. Everything God made, He made by faith. Everything He does, He does by faith. There should be no difference in how you frame your world; what works for God will work for you. The key to shaping your everyday world is understanding faith and living by it. When you act on the Word, you set your faith in motion.

Before a builder erects a house, he must understand some vital information about foundation and framing, or the structure will tumble, and the same concept is true in framing your world with faith. Let's look at three vital areas you must consider as you frame your world with faith; what it is, how to get it, and how to use it.

WHAT IS FAITH?

I imagine some of you are thinking, "Really, Pastor, are you going to revisit the definition of faith again? How many ways and times can you say it in one book?" In this book, I will keep repeating it until THE END. In life, I will continue to speak it until I can speak no more. Faith is so vital; it is my passion that everyone understands and begins to effectively use the power God has entrusted to you in your faith.

Faith is simply believing what God says in His Word. It is trusting what He says more than you trust your natural senses or what other people say. It is an expression of your confidence in God and His Word. Faith is how each and every believer is commanded to live. Hebrews 10:38 is one of the four places God expresses this decree. *"Now the just shall live by faith: but if any man draw back, my soul shall have no pleasure in him"* (KJV). Faith is the foundation and framework of success, and its absence is the cause of failure. God wants you so filled with faith in His Word that your faith becomes bigger in you than the situation. That growing faith causes you to be steadfast and unmovable regardless of what you see or what you hear because your confidence is placed squarely on God.

HOW IS FAITH OBTAINED AND BUILT?

Faith always begins where the will of God is known in a matter. When you know the will of God and get the Word of God on the situation, faith will come. When you begin to focus on the Word, faith develops within your spirit. It will get to a point where the Word becomes the first response of your heart when challenges come. Faith is always available when you need it. It is "on call" to anyone who is willing to submit to the Word of God. Proverbs 4:20–22 (KJV) says, *"My son, attend to my words; incline thine ear unto my sayings. Let them not depart from thine eyes; keep them in the midst of thine heart. For they are life unto those that find them, and health to all their flesh."* You receive God's Word in our heart (spirit) by reading it, speaking it, hearing it, meditating on it, and acting on it.

God's Word causes faith to manifest and rise up within your spirit to draw the promises and provisions of God from the spiritual realm into the natural realm. Romans 10:17 reveals that faith comes by hearing the Word of God, and when the Word is released from your heart with your mouth, it brings the fulfillment of God's promises.

HOW IS FAITH USED?

Faith does not sit around doing nothing. Faith acts! To operate in faith you must **DO** something. Faith is activated when you speak the Word that is alive in your heart. That is when *your* words begin to agree with *God's* Word. Looking to the Father as your example, you find in Genesis that faith is released with words. Words of faith demand results of whatever they say. I know you looked at this earlier in this chapter, but it warrants a relook.

In Genesis 1 (KJV), the account of creation goes something like this, in verses 2–3: *"And the earth was without form, and void; and darkness was upon the face of the deep. And the Spirit of God moved upon the face of the waters. And **God said**, Let there be light: and there was light."* The Spirit of God was moving upon the face of the waters. However, it was not until God spoke and released the substance of His faith that you see creation in manifestation. As God spoke, the Holy Spirit took the substance of faith that resided in God's words and performed what He said. God's words were the instruments that released the faith that framed the worlds. "In the beginning **God said**, Let there be light . . . and there was light. **God said**, Let there be a firmament . . . and it was so. **God said**, Let us make man . . ." Do you see the pattern? God said . . . and it was so. God said . . . and it was so."

Simply agreeing with the Word does not change a thing; you must say what the Word says. God literally spoke all Creation into existence. According to Hebrews 11:3, the worlds were framed by the Word of God. That is the very same way you are to frame your world. You are created in God's image to live like Him and do things as He did! Notice that Genesis does not say "God thought and it was so"; no, God spoke. That is how He operates, that is how faith operates, and that is how you are to operate.

Before this chapter closes, let's take a break for preventative measures. You know even as you operate in this fearless faith, framing your world, shaping your ministry with faith in God and His Word, ask yourself these questions: "Is my trust and confidence in God still strong? Do I approach negative situations with less assurance? Am I bothered or frustrated or overly concerned by things the enemy or life throws my way?" If you said yes to any of these questions, I say grace on you. Even the greatest warrior will become weary in the midst of battle if they do not take precautions.

It is vital that you check yourself from time to time and give others, who are close, opportunities to check you. Continuously assess if you are still walking in fearless faith, framing your world with power through your faith. It is easy to become battle weary and worn. If you find this happening to you, reset your focus. Truthfully evaluate where you are placing your faith and confidence. Are you still **FULLY** relying on God, or are you absorbing some of the burdens for what God said that He would accomplish? Answer yourself truthfully and readjust your focus as necessary. Do not ever quit do not become frustrated with situations or yourself. Remember, Hebrews 10:35 (AMPC) says, *"Do not, therefore, fling away your fearless confidence, for it carries a great and glorious compensation of reward."*

Recall and rejoice in the absolute fact that God is faithful! *"Let us hold fast the profession of our faith without wavering; (for he is faithful that promised)."* Hebrews 10:23 (KJV) With that truth in hand, frame your world with your faith!

Think About It

1. Just as God created with His words, so do you. The question is, what are you creating, victory or defeat?

2. If your faith is weak, you are not spending enough time with God in His Word. The great thing about that fact is you and only you have the ability to make the necessary change.

3. Mentally agreeing with God will not render success, and it will not frame your world with faith. Faith requires action.

4. Has your faith in God diminished in the battle? If the honest answer is yes, reset your focus before you move forward.

Personal Notes

CHAPTER 14

Fully Persuaded Faith

"Yet he did not waver through unbelief regarding the promise of God, but was strengthened in his faith and gave glory to God, being fully persuaded that God had power to do what he had promised." Romans 4:20–21

"*S*o then faith cometh by hearing, and hearing by the word of God."[19] Now, I know that is a very familiar Scripture to most. Sometimes, when something becomes "familiar," people have a tendency of allowing its value to be lessened. This happens naturally in relationships, possessions, people, and Scripture as well. However, in those thirteen little words, the Apostle Paul establishes a foundational truth for every believer who desires to live the victorious life of faith.

FAITH COMES BY HEARING THE WORD OF GOD

You cannot believe the Word unless you first hear the Word. In that hearing, it cannot be an "event" of words passing your ears. This hearing requires interaction with and understanding of the Word you hear. It is impossible to have confidence in that of which you have no knowledge. Think about it, even in relationships, the people you have the greatest confidence in are the people you know, the ones who have proven themselves to be consistently faithful and true. As you hear the Word, faith comes and faith grows within you.

As a believer, there is one area God expects you to always grow in, your faith: your ability to trust Him on another level. You need to realize that your willingness to trust the Lord affects every area of your lives. How you feel, what you see, what you do, the way He blesses you, and whether your prayers are answered are all connected to your growing faith. There is no way you should be continuously walking with God and your faith remains stagnant. He never intended belief and trust to be a onetime event with the single purpose of ushering you into salvation. The older you get in Christ, the greater your test will become; maintaining the same level of faith as a new convert is dangerous. You realize that is not a new concept, it is a lesson children are taught, as they grow older and more mature, responsibility and expectation increase.

GROWING FAITH

A person who is growing in faith is a person who is learning to trust and depend on Christ more and more. Faith, like a muscle, must be exercised to grow stronger. A faith that cannot be tested cannot be trusted. All believers, regardless how long you have been a Christian, must expect their faith to be tried. James 1:2–4 (NKJV) says, *"My brethren, count it all joy when you fall into various trials, knowing that the testing of your faith produces patience. But let patience have its perfect work, that you may be perfect and complete, lacking nothing."* This Scripture is lived out in your life when you face difficulties or heartbreak, and you can see, *naturally*, the impossibility of the circumstances. However, you also see beyond your natural sight to the greatness of your God, and you rejoice. Further, when you are faced with the negative report of others, doubting voices, skeptical advice, and the lies of satan; yet above all the clatter, you hear the voice of Truth, and you begin to celebrate victory and success, that it is then you are putting visual life to God's Word! Those who choose to believe what God says experience the peace and joy of knowing He has everything under His control. This is the result of growing faith.

3-LEVEL GAUGE

When looking at growing faith, there are three levels to gauge where you stand: little faith, great faith, and perfect faith.

- **Little Faith** – This stage is characterized by struggling to believe God. You hope He will answer your prayer, but you are just not sure. At every turn, doubt slithers in as you focus on the situation versus the Lord and His Word. Little faith is experienced by people who do not truly understand what God has said in the Bible. Believers who are new in their relationship with Christ or otherwise uneducated in God's Word often fall into this category. They have nothing to anchor their faith (Matthew 6:30–33).

- **Great Faith** – This phase can also be called "stretching faith" because it involves stretching to believe the Lord more and more. It is at this level Christians begin to stand on the truth of scripture. It is here you begin to permit the Word of God to shape your thinking and petitions, trusting He will grant your requests (Matthew 8:5–10).

- **Perfect Faith** – This should be the goal of Christians; perfect and mature faith. This is the level of faith that allows you to rest in confidence, knowing that the Lord has already accomplished what you have asked. When your requests align with His, you will know "it is a done deal." At this point you take a position of gratitude and worship with earnest expectation as you wait for His promise to become a manifested reality (James 2:22).

God's Word, alive and active in your life, is what fuels the rising through these three levels of faith. It is a process that will usher you into fully persuaded faith. Faith that stands in the face of anything with assurance and complete confidence that not only is your God able, but He is willing. Some of you may be thinking, Now, Pastor, you forgot the title of this chapter is Fully Persuaded Faith, not

Growing Your Faith. No, I did not forget the title; I am right where I should be. You see faith that is not fully grown cannot be fully persuaded.

THE RESULT OF DEEP CONVICTION

The phrase "fully persuaded" in Greek means completely assured, fully convinced; to carry through to the end; seeing things already accomplished; to cause someone to adopt a certain position or belief.[20] The Bible declares that Abraham was fully persuaded, assured of, and convinced that God was able to do what He promised **AND** that He would do it. What does Numbers 23:19 (NKJV) reveal about God? *"God is not a man, that He should lie, Nor a son of man, that He should repent. Has He said, and will He not do? Or has He spoken, and will He not make it good?"* Just like Abraham was fully convinced and persuaded that God would do what He promised and that He was able to perform it, in your heart you too need that same persuasion, that deep conviction. Look at Romans 14:5b (KJV): *"Let every man be fully persuaded in his own mind."* When you arrive at a point where you earnestly believe and embrace truth as truth and begin living your day to day life in line with that belief, you will be living a fully persuaded life. That kind of living will lead to victorious living!

Let me tell you three incredible results that come from living a life of deep conviction and being fully persuaded in your faith in God.

- Deep conviction enables you to handle difficult times and situations without giving up.

- Deep conviction helps you to stay true and hold fast to the promise until the manifestation shows up.

- Deep conviction allows you to rest in God patiently.

Abraham understood the character of God; he believed God and refused to entertain doubt. He refused to distrust, stagger, or waiver, he just kept his faith switch turned on. Romans 4:21 (KJV) says of Abraham's faith, *"And being fully persuaded that, what he had promised, he was able also to perform."* Faith is a principle instrument that you must use to do great and mighty exploits in Christ despite what is seen; and that is a key factor observed in the life of Abraham. He understood God stands ready to perform His Word (Jeremiah 1:12); and Abraham lived a life that totally reflected his fully persuaded faith—his deep conviction.

- <u>Mary</u> was fully persuaded (Luke 1:34–38, 45).

- <u>Joseph</u> was fully persuaded (Genesis 37–45 and 50).

- <u>The woman with the issue of blood</u> was fully persuaded (Mark 5:28–34).

- <u>Blind Bartimaeus</u> was fully persuaded (Mark 10:46–53).

- <u>Elijah</u> was fully persuaded (1 Kings 17:8–24).

- <u>Daniel, Shadrach, Meshach and Adeb-Nego</u> were fully persuaded (Daniel 3:16–27).

- <u>Richard Peoples</u> is fully persuaded.

_____ is fully persuaded. Can you truthfully fill your name in that line? Keep in mind, it is a process; a process that will require you to spend time in His presence and in His Word. Remember, do not allow others to talk you out of or cause you to waiver in your faith-filled conviction of what God has assured you. Living a life of fully persuaded faith is the only way to live a victorious life for the rest of your life.

Think About It

1. When you are living the fully persuaded life, you believe God will do what He said He will do; no matter how long it takes.

2. You will not be moved by what you see when you are living the fully persuaded life.

3. When you are living the fully persuaded life, you will be "steadfast, immovable and always abounding in the work of the Lord." 1 Corinthians 15:58 (NASB)

4. When you are living the fully persuaded life you know God will *"do exceedingly abundantly above all that we ask or think, according to the power that works in us."* Ephesians 3:20–21 (NKJV)

Personal Notes

CHAPTER 15

Faith for Life

*"Yet he did not waver through unbelief regarding the
promise of God, but was strengthened in his faith and gave
glory to God, being fully persuaded that God had power
to do what he had promised." Romans 4:20–21*

Through God's leading, I have shared much over the past
fourteen chapters. In this final chapter, it is my assignment
to pull all of that together while sharing a few more
principles that will give you the power to embrace faith for life,
which will lead to a victorious life of faith.

The core or empowering truth to your faith is an individual
understanding and acceptance of the simple yet profound truth
that God is for you and not against you. I would like to assume
that by Chapter 15, you have that truth securely locked in, but I
find that assumption is often dangerous. So if for only one person,
let's take a few lines to reiterate this truth.

GOD IS FOR YOU—NOT AGAINST YOU

Look at Deuteronomy 20:1–4. *"When you go to war against your
enemies and see horses and chariots and an army greater than yours, do
not be afraid of them, because the Lord your God who brought you up
out of Egypt will be with you. When you are about to go into battle,
the priest shall come forward and address the army. He shall say: 'Hear,
Israel: Today you are going into battle against your enemies. Do not
be fainthearted or afraid; do not panic or be terrified by them. For*

the Lord your God is the one who goes with you to fight for you against your enemies to give you victory.'" Let's also look at a reference in Romans 8:31–32. *"What, then, shall we say in response to these things? If God is for us, who can be against us? He who did not spare his own Son, but gave him up for us all—how will he not also, along with him, graciously give us all things?"*

Do you see in these example Scriptures, of many, that God is for you and not against you? God's love for you and your victory go hand in hand. Those who are living a victorious life of faith understand the truth that God is for you. Those of you who are struggling and wavering have allowed the enemy to infiltrate your thinking with fear and doubt, considering the lie that God is against you. Fear will paralyze your faith. Faith for life requires that you always trust and believe that God loves you. Even as you face difficulties, heart break, death of loved ones, financial catastrophe, debilitating health challenges—faith for life must rise above the pain and distress, calling out louder than other calls reminding you that God is for you! I wish I could say that your life of faith will shield you from the challenges I just named, but that would be a lie; a lie that would ultimately cause you to doubt God and His love for you. Truth, however, is truth and Jesus expressed this reality as He warned and encouraged believers in John 16:33: *"I have told you these things, so that in Me you may have [perfect] peace. In the world you have tribulation and distress and suffering, but be courageous [be confident, be undaunted, be filled with joy]; I have overcome the world [My conquest is accomplished, My victory abiding.]"* (AMP). After Jesus revealed this "hard saying," the next thing He did was pray, for Himself, His disciples, and all believers. He knew to live life with an understanding that trials will come, but the victory is assured would call for great faith; faith in God and faith for life.

There is a connection between life and faith. The life of God or the life God has planned for you can only be received by grace through faith. Remember God's Word teaches how believers are to live this life; not by education, status, paycheck, or who you have on speed dial. You are called to live your life by faith.[21] Jesus is your example in this, and as His followers, you are expected to carry on in the same manner. Yes, it is possible. After all, what does God reveal through 2 Corinthians 4:13? *"It is written: 'I believed; therefore I have spoken.' Since we have that same spirit of faith, we also believe and therefore speak."* You have the same spirit of faith that your Savior had in Him, therefore, living like He lived—by faith—is very possible!

HAVE FAITH IN GOD

Should you live by faith in select areas of our life? Should you allow what you see and what you hear to alter your steps and plans as established by God? Absolutely not! In every area at all times, you are to *"walk by faith and not by sight."*[22] In other words, challenges should cause you to practically and visually express the confidence you have in God and His Word. Recall what Jesus said to His disciples in Mark 11:22 as they saw the withered fig tree: *"Have faith in God."* Now, with all you know about Jesus, do you think if faith in God was not available to all believers, at all times, in all situations He would have issued this mandate? I do not think so either; it is not His character to give an impossible assignment. God is not the God of disappointment—there is no glory to His name in your failure.

DO NOT DOUBT

In the next verse, Jesus warns you to guard yourself against doubt. *"I assure you and most solemnly say to you, whoever says to this mountain, 'Be lifted up and thrown into the sea!' and does not doubt in his heart [in God's unlimited power], but believes that what he says is going to take place, it will be done for him [in accordance with God's will]"* (Mark 11:23, AMP). Jesus said do not doubt "God's unlimited power." In this life of faith, doubt will always be a looming adversary sent to cause you to stagger and waiver (both words synonymous with doubt).

"If any of you lacks wisdom, you should ask God, who gives generously to all without finding fault, and it will be given to you. But when you ask, you must believe and not doubt, because the one who doubts is like

a wave of the sea, blown and tossed by the wind. That person should not expect to receive anything from the Lord. Such a person is double-minded and unstable in all they do" (James 1:5–8). When you are wavering, you are both staggering and doubting. You are moving with whatever circumstances you are facing or that are surrounding you. Vacillating, instability, and wavering will prevent you from receiving from God. Doubting, double-minded, or standing in two ways is a favorite tool of the enemy because he knows its destructive ability. Embrace faith for life—do not doubt.

THE ANSWER NEVER CHANGES

Faith for life will always have the same answer to challenges and situations… the answer will never change - **Have Faith in God**. People throughout the world are looking for answers and solutions and the answer is - **Have Faith in God**. No matter what is going on, regardless of what the situation looks, like the answer is the answer that was given over two thousand years ago as *"Jesus replied, 'Have faith in God [constantly].'"*[23] The security and power of having faith in God never changes because God never changes; He is the same yesterday, today, and forever![24] Faith always gives God access into your life; an opening through which He can funnel all His favor, grace, and blessings.

Having faith in God will encompass having faith in His Word and faith in His love. A believer's faith in God will be seen by others as absolute confidence in God as revealed in behavior. In other words, your belief, your faith will be seen in your actions; whatever you believe you will act on that belief.

Faith for life is God's desire for every believer. After all, without faith it is impossible to please Him and my desire and your desire is to live a victorious life of faith that is pleasing to our Heavenly Father.

God loves you. God is for you. Embrace that truth forever, it will usher you into *The Victorious Life of Faith!*

Think About It

1. God is for you. No matter what situations you face remind yourself: "God is for me."

2. Before the battle, set yourself, no matter what you see or what you hear, to live a life of faith.

3. To obtain the fullness of what God has predestined for you, you must operate in faith.

4. Doubt is a weapon of mass destruction used by the enemy. The only weapon capable of neutralizing it is your faith in God.

Personal Notes

END NOTES

1   Blue Letter Bible, "Greek Lexicon," https://www.blueletterbible.org/lang/lexicon/lexicon.cfm?Strongs=G2222&t=KJV.
2   Heb. 11:6.
3   Hab. 2:4, Rom. 1:17, Gal. 3:11, and Heb. 10:38.
4   Matt. 17:20 KJV.
5   Google search, "Confidence," google.com.
6   Hab. 2:4, Rom. 1:17, Gal. 3:11, and Heb. 10:38.
7   John 20:24–29.
8   Blue Letter Bible, www.blueletterbible.org.
9   Blue Letter Bible, "Greek Lexicon," https://www.blueletterbible.org/lang/Lexicon/Lexicon.cfm?strongs=G1343&t=KJV 2/18/2016.
10 Heb. 12:2.
11 Hab. 2:4, Rom. 1:17, Gal. 3:11, and He. 10:38.
12 Dictionary.com, "unbeatable," http://dictionary.reference.com/browse/unbeatable.
13 Merriam Webster Dictionary, "genuine," http://www.merriam-webster.com/dictionary/genuine.
14 2 Cor. 5:7.
15 James 1:6–8.
16 1 Sam. 17.
17 Rom. 10:17.
18 Merriam Webster Dictionary, "confidence," http://www.merriam-webster.com/dictionary/confidence.
19 Rom. 10:17 KJV.
20 Bible Hub, "Thayer's Greek Lexicon," http://biblehub.com/greek/4135.htm.
21 Hab. 2:4, Rom. 1:17, Gal. 3:11, and Heb. 10:38.
22 2 Cor. 5:7.
23 Mark 11:22 AMP.
24 Heb. 13:8.

Edwards Brothers Malloy
Thorofare, NJ USA
October 24, 2016